Praise for *Pinfluence*

"To grow your business in today's new media world, you must create content in the social networks where your customers are. Pinterest is the newest such network, and it has grown quickly to rival Twitter and YouTube in some markets. In her new book, the first on Pinterest marketing, Beth Hayden shows you how to use this powerful new network to reach your buyers precisely when they are looking for what you have to offer."

—David Meerman Scott, bestselling author of *The New Rules of Marketing and PR*

"Beth Hayden has written the definitive guide to Pinterest for real-world businesses. If you're unclear on how to turn Pinterest from a 'fun time-waster' to a valuable business tool, you need this book."

—Sonia Simone, Copyblogger Media

"If you're a marketer, you don't need another article about how to post cute photos to Pinterest. You need a comprehensive plan for reaching the right people in just the right way and transforming them into customers. That's what *Pinfluence* is."

—Jon Morrow, associate editor of Copyblogger and founder of Boost Blog Traffic

"My excitement about marketing opportunities with Pinterest, the hot new property on the social media scene, was tempered with being overwhelmed about how to actually use the darn thing. Thank goodness Beth Hayden created this clear, useful, and pragmatic guide to help business owners tap into this bustling, vibrant, and lucrative market. I am hooked!"

—Pamela Slim, author of *Escape from Cubicle Nation: From Corporate Prisoner to Thriving Entrepreneur*

"Pinterest has captured people's hearts in a way that no other social platform has done in recent years. The visual experience you will receive on Pinterest is completely addicting, and that is the reason for its explosive growth. Beth Hayden does an incredible job walking you through the ins and outs of Pinterest so you know exactly how to tap into Pinterest for business. Use Pinterest the right way and your website will see massive traffic. Use it the wrong way and you will turn off your potential customers and clients. Beth is a true Pinterest expert and power user, and I highly recommend this book for anyone looking to take advantage of the web's hottest platform."

—Andrea Vahl of www.AndreaVahl.com and Community Manager at www.SocialMediaExaminer.com

"Beth is a nationally recognized blogging and social media coach, and it's no surprise that she has turned her attention to helping businesses leverage Pinterest, the web's latest viral phenomenon. Unlike casual references available on the market, *Pinfluence* gives readers a comprehensive deep dive into the marketing power of Pinterest and teaches them step-by-step how to leverage Pinterest as part of a profitable social media strategy."

—Holly Hamann, VP of Marketing and co-founder of BlogFrog

"It's important for all business owners to take social media seriously if they want to stay ahead in their industry. Pinterest is a powerful tool for driving massive traffic to websites and blogs and *a must* for staying ahead of your competitors and in tune with your audience. Let *Pinfluence* be your guide to fully understanding how to maximize this powerful social network."

—Lewis Howes, entrepreneur and author of *The Ultimate Webinar Marketing Guide*

"Avoid all the common mistakes trying to tap into the visual world of Pinterest for your business marketing efforts by studying Beth's terrific *Pinfluence* book. It's certainly helped me become a popular and effective Pinner!"

—Dave Taylor, www.AskDaveTaylor.com

"I'm relatively new to the beautiful world of Pinterest. Beth Hayden's book showed me that it can be about more than pinning pretty things to boards. Done right, Pinterest is a way of building community."

—Shauna James Ahern, author and award-winning blogger at Gluten-Free Girl, and the Chef, www.glutenfreegirl.com

"Finally, a book on social media with actual revenue-producing ideas instead of the hazy 'social proof' benefits touted by so many others. Avoid the social media time suck and get focused with Beth's creative and doable suggestions. Beth is your Pinterest muse, magician, and moneymaker. Pay close attention to learn how pretty pictures can generate more revenue for your business."

—Betsy Talbot, author and blogger, Married with Luggage, www.marriedwithluggage.com

"I'm overflowing with ideas after reading *Pinfluence*! Beth Hayden shares loads of uses for business that I'm already starting to implement. My artist-clients, who love Pinterest's visual platform, are going to inhale this book. It will be the go-to guide for any business wanting to make the most of Pinterest's popularity."

—Alyson B. Stanfield, founder of ArtBizCoach.com and ArtBizBlog.com

"For the longest time, I didn't 'get' Pinterest. I thought it was just the latest social media fad—exciting today and forgotten tomorrow. Then I read *Pinfluence*, and my perspective changed in a huge way. Suddenly, my imagination was captivated by Pinterest's enormous potential for reaching prospects and customers through the platform, and my mind was racing with ideas for how to leverage it all to get results with my own business. Read *Pinfluence*, and you'll feel the same way."

—Danny Iny, Firepole Marketing

"*Pinfluence* is the online marketer's best new reference on how to leverage the Pinterest phenomenon. Beth's done a fabulous job of capturing both the high-level and nitty-gritty details every small business pinner needs to know to be successful. Grab this book and get pinning!"

—Tea Silvestre, small business marketing consultant and author of *Attract and Feed a Hungry Crowd*

Pinfluence

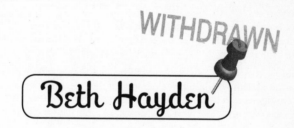

THE COMPLETE GUIDE TO
**MARKETING YOUR BUSINESS
WITH PINTEREST**

Beth Hayden

WILEY

John Wiley & Sons, Inc.

Published by John Wiley & Sons, Inc., Hoboken, New Jersey.
Published simultaneously in Canada.

For general information on our other products and services or for technical support, please contact our Customer Care Department within the United States at (800) 762-2974, outside the United States at (317) 572-3993 or fax (317) 572-4002.

Wiley publishes in a variety of print and electronic formats and by print-on-demand. Some material included with standard print versions of this book may not be included in e-books or in print-on-demand. If this book refers to media such as a CD or DVD that is not included in the version you purchased, you may download this material at http://booksupport. wiley.com. For more information about Wiley products, visit www.wiley.com.

Library of Congress Cataloging-in-Publication Data:

Hayden, Beth, 1975-
    Pinfluence : the complete guide to marketing your business with Pinterest / Beth Hayden.
       p. cm.
    Includes index.
    ISBN 978-1-118-39377-2 (pbk.); ISBN 978-1-118-41468-2 (ebk);
    ISBN 978-1-118-41469-9 (ebk); ISBN 978-1-118-41471-2 (ebk)
       1. Internet marketing–Social aspects.   2. Pinterest.   3. Web sites–Design.
    I. Title.
    HF5415.1265.H386   2012
    658.8'72—dc23
                                                                2012015127

Printed in the United States of America
10 9 8 7 6 5 4 3 2 1

For Ben, the light of my life.

Contents

Introduction

In the last few years, social media has evolved from a cutting-edge technique to an essential aspect of any company's marketing strategy. Companies in today's business climate can no longer afford to ignore Internet marketing strategies that help them interact with their clients and listen to their feedback online. Businesses need to embrace the world of social media, or they will not survive.

This is the marketing scene that spawned Pinterest, a social networking tool that allows users to create and share images or videos by creating digital *pinboards*—a collection of so-called *pins*, usually with a common theme.

Pinterest launched in 2009 and initially gained some traction with women in the United States. Although people were using the tool, it seemed as though Pinterest was a closely guarded secret that only a select few individuals—mostly, people planning weddings or weekly recipes—were utilizing. Pinterest had not yet reached its tipping point.

Even though they were still in closed beta, invitation-only mode, Pinterest hit its stride at the end of 2011 and started growing at an extraordinary rate. The web was aflutter with news of celebrities, politicians, and other high-profile users who seemed to love Pinterest as much as their beloved In-and-Out Burger.

The site reported more than 10 million unique monthly visitors in January 2012, and social media sites jubilantly published Pinterest stats proclaiming that Pinterest had reached the 10-million-visitor mark faster than almost any social media site in history.

And Pinterest's increasing numbers are showing no signs of slowing. Every day seems to bring news of another traffic or popularity record that Pinterest has broken.

Even more interesting to those who were keeping a close eye on how the business drama was unfolding was the fact that Pinterest's referral traffic numbers were far exceeding expectations.

In January 2012, Pinterest drove more traffic to websites and blogs than YouTube, Google+, and LinkedIn *combined*, according to content-sharing site Shareaholic.[1] Then in February 2012, Pinterest shocked the world by bypassing Twitter in terms of referral traffic. Clearly, the cat was out of the bag—and that cat was a gold mine for businesses.[2]

Case studies of businesses and blogs who received an avalanche of traffic from Pinterest began circulating on the web, with each story seemingly more incredible than the last.

And an even more important fact: Pinterest users are buying. A survey from PriceGrabber stated that 21 percent of Pinterest users purchased something they saw on a pinboard. Marketers all over the world heard this statistic and quietly imagined the sound of cash registers ringing up sales.[3]

What Does All This Mean for You as a Business Owner?

Beyond all the hype, Pinterest truly is a huge business opportunity for you. The site has proven itself to be incredibly powerful and addictive—and very valuable to business owners looking to market themselves online.

Pinterest unleashes the inner scrapbooker in all of us—the part of us that wants to create visually stunning things and share

---

[1] http://blog.shareaholic.com/2012/01/pinterest-referral-traffic.
[2] http://blog.shareaholic.com/2012/03/pinterest-referral-traffic-2.
[3] http://thenextweb.com/insider/2012/03/28/survey-21-of-users-on-pinterest-have-purchased-an-item-that-they-found-on-the-site.

them with the world. You can think of Pinterest as a huge room where people gather with collections of their favorite things— all of the *stuff* they find interesting. They gather to add to their collections, but also to find like-minded people who enjoy the same things they do.

Pinterest's system is simple. You *pin* images and videos to online collages that you create on various topics. Each pin links to the source of the image or video, whether it's a blog post, article, catalog page, or other web page that gives you more information about that pin. It's simple and easy.

Pinterest's value, however, might be harder to initially spot. Marketers might look at Pinterest's lovely images of fashion, wedding venues, and recipes and think, "This can't possibly be useful for me." But you'd be surprised what you can do with images and pinboards. There's a whole world of visual marketing that businesses can dive into with Pinterest.

As Pinterest began to catch on, brands and businesses took notice. There was the predictable avalanche of blog posts and articles about how to use Pinterest for business purposes. My goal with this book is to spotlight some of the *best* marketing ideas and put them together in one easy reference that you can pull out and use whenever you need.

I've been a social media expert since 2005, and I teach entrepreneurs and business owners how to make more money and engage with their clients using content-rich websites, social media marketing, and video campaigns. With all my clients, in every situation, I teach them the all-important tenets of content marketing (which we'll talk about in depth later in this book).

Ever since I joined Pinterest, I've spent many hours pinning and repinning images to a growing number of useful pinboards. I won't lie; Pinterest is great fun. I love using it.

But Pinterest also provides other benefits. It helps me connect with my target audience and kick off discussions on topics that are central to my business. It allows me to get a sneak peek into the inner lives of my ideal clients, to find out what's going on in their homes, gardens, kitchens, and offices, and discover what their values are. And it helps me provide great content for my followers (helping me practice the content marketing principles I preach to my clients).

Pinterest has also helped me build relationships with my referral partners, colleagues, and customers. And as of right now, Pinterest is also the number-two driver of traffic to my business website.

This book is written for business owners, marketers, PR representatives, and bloggers who are trying to grow their businesses. It's also for nonprofit employees, writers, changemakers, and anyone else who has a message to amplify or a mission to carry out in the world.

In short, if you need to tell the world about what you do—if you need to reach people—this book is for you.

Overview

The book's first sections will explain what you can do to get the most out of Pinterest, and how to make the pinning process—publishing images and videos to online pinboards—work for your company. I'll start with an introduction to Pinterest, and why it should be an important part of your online marketing strategy.

Then I'll walk you through the process of creating a solid, powerful Pinterest profile and starting to create pins and boards that will act as the foundation for your Pinterest marketing work. You'll come out of these chapters knowing how to get an account, set up a proper profile, create your Pinterest brand strategy, set up boards, pin and repin images, and get into conversations in the Pinterest user interface.

Next, we'll dive into practical aspects of Pinterest marketing techniques, including great content creation, how to optimize websites and blogs for pinning, and how to start growing your followers. You will also learn how to integrate Pinterest with other social media tools (including Facebook and Twitter, as well as your blog) and how to track trends and monitor conversation on Pinterest.

The last section of the book will cover more advanced Pinterest marketing techniques, including more ways to engage with followers and grow your audience, how to use the Pinterest iPhone app, and advice for special types of businesses (i.e., B2B companies and nonprofits). The book will conclude with a section on Pinterest copyright issues, diving into the thorny world of Pinterest ethics.

Throughout the book, you'll get action checklists and advice on how to avoid wasting time on Pinterest. It is critical that you learn how to convert Pinterest followers (and visitors to your website that come from Pinterest) into active buyers and customers.

Of course, there is no single, one-size-fits-all recipe for success on Pinterest. My goal is to give you lots of ideas for marketing in a creative and compelling way using this new social platform; however, not *all* of the ideas I discuss will work for you. I'd like you to come out of this book with a strong grasp on how Pinterest works so that it will spark ideas for your marketing team, customer service team, or fundraising group.

You can enter Pinterest's dynamic and interesting room of scrapbookers and collectors, and if you're smart and considerate, you can use Pinterest as a powerful marketing tool to grow your business, make more money, and build powerful, loyal communities around your brand.

Part One

Getting Started

Why Pinterest?

Ana White started her blog (ana-white.com) in 2009 as a way to share her love of woodworking with other people. The site began as a way for her to share plans for building furniture, including the beautiful bed frame she created for her own house. She posted photos and ideas for new projects, as well as stories about her family life in rural Alaska, on her blog every single day.

Now White's blog attracts *nearly three million page views every month*. And while those traffic numbers alone are cause for surprise, the source of that traffic might shock you even more.

Pinterest is White's number-one source of traffic, bringing her site 6,000 unique visitors every day. By its second year, this Alaska mom's blog began bringing in enough advertising revenue to support her entire family.[1]

Pinterest is the perfect platform for White's blog. Her furniture plans and home photos get passed around like wildfire on the image-sharing site, and users share her posts with their friends as they plan their next projects. You can check out her pinning strategy at @antiquewhite.

White's story of success—with her blog, and with Pinterest—is truly remarkable, and her designs and products are wonderfully crafted. However, I share her story not merely to expose you to a talented artist, but also to give you a glimpse of what is possible with Pinterest. Done authentically and well, Pinterest marketing can be a powerful source of traffic to your website, and can help you build an incredible community of followers and superfans who loyally support everything you do.

---

[1]www.socialmediaexaminer.com/how-alaskan-mom-brings-millions-to-her-carpentry-blog.

The Appeal of Pinterest

Ben Silbermann, one of Pinterest's co-founders, was apparently a meticulous collector who, as a child, kept glass boxes full of beetles and stamps. It was this collector mindset that generated the inspiration for Pinterest. Silbermann noted that the simple act of collecting is universal, and he wanted to build a site that made the act of online collecting—and sharing these collections—easy and fun.[2] Pinterest's ability to indulge the inner collector in all of us is likely part of the reason why the site is so addictive.

Dr. Christopher Long teaches a course on consumer psychology at Ouachita Baptist University, and explains it in the following way: "Pinterest boards are like its users' personal happiness collages," he says. "[They represent] things that I appreciate, that I desire, and that express who I am, whether the things are cupcakes, shirtless David Beckham, or an inspirational quotation."[3]

Chelsea Smith, the Social Media Specialist for Oreck, reported that her CEO asked her to set up a Pinterest account for the company after he'd gone on a family vacation to Mexico and noticed something surprising on the trip. He observed that every woman in his travel party was "more interested in Pinterest than getting tans and drinking margaritas!" He admitted that he wasn't 100 percent sure what the site was all about, but he observed, "This is big. We've got to get on this!" Smith had already started a Pinterest account for the vacuum cleaner company, and was given the go-ahead to dive into planning extensive Oreck Pinterest campaigns.

Addictive? Yes. Brilliant marketing for Oreck? Absolutely.

Smart companies are all getting on Pinterest these days, especially now that it has become a proven source of traffic and

---

[2]www.nytimes.com/2012/03/12/technology/start-ups/pinterest-aims-at-the-scrapbook-maker-in-all-of-us.html?_r=3&pagewanted=1 (March 11, 2012).
[3]www.fastcompany.com/1816603/why-pinterest-is-so-addictive.

conversions for the websites that embrace it. And your company should be following their lead.

The Pinterest Audience

You've likely heard by now that most of the current Pinterest user base is made up of women. While reports on the exact statistics differ, most researchers claim that approximately 60 percent of U.S. Pinterest users are female, most between 25 and 34 years old.

Yet there's nothing inherently female-centric about the site; it is essentially an image-sharing service that lets people collect their favorite stuff from the web. At its onset, Pinterest happened to have caught on particularly well with a young female demographic group. But as the site continues to grow, there is no reason to believe it won't also attract lots of men. It's already starting to attract male gadget lovers and home improvement aficionados by the score.

Social Media Strategist Mike Street (@mikestreet), for example, manages a great collection of male-friendly pins on a board called "BroPin." His board, which is a collaborative collage maintained by more than 35 men, includes over 800 images of clothing, cars, technology, and food that specifically appeal to guys. And Ben Golder (@beng), an ecological architecture design student from Barcelona who has nearly 200,000 followers, curates male-friendly boards about robotics and architecture.

Pinterest also has a growing user base in other parts of the world, and the gender mix in those countries is quite different from that in the U.S. For example, Pinterest gets about 200,000 unique visitors each month from the United Kingdom, and the majority of those British visitors (56 percent) are male.

So don't let anyone tell you that Pinterest is just a *chick thing*, or that it's only good for advertising in women-friendly industries like weddings and fashion. We'll talk later about ways to use Pinterest for non-profits and B2B companies, too; but realize that Pinterest is a flexible, friendly, easy-to-use tool that can have enormous benefits for a great variety of businesses—and customers.

Why Pinterest?

So why should *you* use Pinterest for marketing? The following are some reasons why smart and effective companies are harnessing Pinterest to attract new leads, drive traffic to their websites, and engage with their customers:

- **Pinterest can be an important part of your content marketing strategy.** Content is still king in the online world, and Pinterest's visual content can really help to round out your online strategy. Publishing great content via blogs, social media sites, and image-sharing sites like Pinterest helps you attract new customers and develop great relationships with your current ones. And if your content is really outstanding, those customers and followers will share your brand's message *for* you. What more could you ask for?

- **People are making buying decisions based on what they see in social media.** Massachusetts-based marketing software company HubSpot reported in January 2012 that individuals are 71 percent *more likely* to make a purchase when a product or service has been recommended by a friend via social media. Smart businesses are making sure that their products are easy to find and recommend on social media sites like Pinterest.[4]

- **Humanizing your brand.** Pinterest's visual nature makes it a great way to give customers (and potential customers) a glimpse into the heart of your brand, and what your

[4]http://blog.hubspot.com/blog/tabid/6307/bid/30239/71-More-Likely-to-Purchase-Based-on-Social-Media-Referrals-Infographic.aspx.

company stands for. The more you let your brand's per-sonality come through in your pinboards, the more human you can be—and the more successful you will be with Pinterest.

- **It can act as a constant source of inspiration for you.** No matter what industry you're in, interacting on Pinterest and looking at great content can be a terrific source of inspiration. Artists, photographers, and other creative pro-fessionals use Pinterest as a sort of online muse—and you can, too!

- **You can use it to grow your platform.** As a collector and curator of interesting things on Pinterest, you'll attract like-minded people who enjoy the same things that you—and your company—do. You can use Pinterest to build a strong, lively, engaged community, whether you want to use that platform to sell books, advertise coaching services, or pitch your book to a big publisher. With a great platform, the sky's the limit!

Now that you've seen all the reasons why Pinterest market-ing is a great choice for modern businesses, let's walk through the first steps of building your presence on Pinterest—starting with how to build a powerful business Pinterest profile.

Where Do You Start?

Creating a Powerful Profile

Pinterest is simple and easy to use, and it only takes a few minutes to get started. As you're having fun setting up your account with this cool new tool, you can also take some steps to ensure that you establish an excellent foundation for your company's Pinterest success.

In this chapter, I'm going to show you how to set up a powerful groundwork for your Pinterest marketing efforts. I'll explain how the registration process works, advise you on how to decide which options you'll use to set up your account, and walk you through the process of establishing a compelling and useful profile.

First things first—you'll need to get an account invitation. Since Pinterest is currently invitation-only, you'll either need to request an invitation from Pinterest directly, or get a current member to invite you. The response time from the site can vary; some people who request invitations seem to receive them right away, while others wait longer—sometimes even weeks.

Therefore, the quickest and most straightforward way to get an invitation is to ask a friend or colleague with a Pinterest account to send you one. It's easy for a current member to invite their friends. They just have to log in to their Pinterest account, click on their profile name in the upper right, and click the "Invite Friends" option that appears in the drop-down menu. They can then select Facebook friends to invite, or send direct e-mail invitations by clicking "Email" on the left side of the screen. You should get your invitation shortly thereafter.

Once you've been invited, click on the link in your invitation email, and you'll see a big welcome screen that gives you several options for setting up your Pinterest account.

Linking to Facebook or Twitter: Which Should You Do?

You'll find that you have to make a decision even before you get started with Pinterest, as you must connect your account to either your Facebook or your Twitter profile. This is simply so that you can activate Pinterest's social media sharing functions, which help you build your platform. Of course, this begs the question: Which one should you choose?

There are potential benefits and drawbacks to each. When you sign up with Facebook, Pinterest will search through your friends and automatically sign you up to follow any friend who has a Pinterest account. This can be a great way to jump-start your Pinterest following, since many of the people you follow will also follow you back. But using Facebook might not work for your business if you don't use your personal Facebook profile for business purposes, or if you have other reasons that make it difficult or inappropriate for you to link your individual profile to your Pinterest account.

You can also link your Twitter account to your Pinterest profile, which is a good option if you have a Twitter account that you use for business marketing. However, if you only have a personal Twitter profile that you'd rather not link to your Pinterest account, you can always start a new Twitter profile specifically for marketing purposes, and use that for your Pinterest presence.

You do need to choose one of your social media profiles (Twitter or Facebook) to be the initial link to your Pinterest account. But as we'll discover in Chapter 9, there are easy ways to integrate your Pinterest campaigns with both Facebook and Twitter as you are pinning and creating boards—so don't worry that choosing one or the other will limit your social media sharing options on Pinterest.

Once you've weighed the pros and cons, choose the option that feels right for you and your business. If you're not already signed in to your Facebook or Twitter account, you'll need to sign in. Then you'll be asked to authorize Pinterest to access your Facebook or Twitter account. You should know that *granting Pinterest this access will not compromise your password or security.*

If you're using Twitter to create your account, you'll be asked to create your Pinterest username. Your username must be less than 15 characters, so you'll need to keep it brief. Your username will become part of your Pinterest profile URL, and other users will be able to see it. Therefore, you don't want to choose anything too personal, embarrassing, or potentially compromising.

If you know you'll be using Pinterest exclusively for marketing your company, and you want to use your business name as your username, that's great! It's also fine to use your first and last names as your username, too. Nordstrom's department store, for example, uses the Pinterest username @Nordstrom.

If you'd like to use Pinterest as an individual AND as a business, and you really want to keep the two worlds separate, you could consider starting two separate Pinterest accounts. You could accomplish this by starting one account with your Facebook profile and the other with your Twitter account. I would think carefully before doing this, however. Having two Pinterest accounts means twice the effort and twice the maintenance time, so if it's possible for you to just maintain one account, I would recommend it. Also keep in mind that your business followers will enjoy seeing some personal pins from you—it helps them get to know you better and trust you more—so in most cases, there's no reason to hide your personal pins from your business fans.

You'll also need to enter the email address you'd like to use for all your Pinterest communication. Keep in mind that because of the way Pinterest works, you will likely get a *lot* of Pinterest-related emails. So you probably want to choose an email account that will be able to manage a high level of communication without being annoying. You might consider having a dedicated

Pinterest email account for your company, if that makes sense for you and your business.

Finally, choose your password and click on "Create Account." On the next few screens, Pinterest will ask you to select a few topics you're interested in. This just allows the site to make some content recommendations to help you get started. You'll then be prompted to create some initial boards. Pinboards (or just *boards*) are groups of pins; we'll talk about them in more depth in Chapter 3. At this point, you should feel free to agree to Pinterest's default options—and add your own ideas, as well.

After a few more administrative notifications and suggestions from Pinterest, you'll be prompted to click on the "Start Pinning!" button at the bottom of your screen. Now you officially have a Pinterest account that you can use to start personalizing your presence to reflect your brand and your business goals!

Creating a Powerful Profile

You can hover your mouse over your name in the upper right from any page in the Pinterest interface to view a dropdown menu that includes all your account options. Click on "Settings" to view and edit your Pinterest profile (shown in Figure 2.1).

Think carefully about how you set up your Pinterest profile; this is the first impression you'll make on other Pinterest users—people with the potential to become fans and followers. Your Pinterest profile can also serve as a vital link to your website, Facebook profile, and Twitter presence, so take your time working on this!

Profile Name

The very first field on your profile page presents an interesting dilemma for business owners: do you want to use your personal name or your business name when you interact on Pinterest?

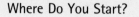

Search 🔍   'Pinterest   Add +   About ▾   🖼

Edit Profile

Email	beth@bloggingwithbeth.com	Not shown publicly
Notifications	**Change Email Settings**	
Password	**Change Password**	
First name	Beth	
Last name	Hayden	
Username	bethhayden	http://pinterest.com/username
Gender	⊖ Male ⦿ Female ○ Unspecified	
About	I pin geeky, blog-related or just plain fun things that educate, inspire and entertain. www.bloggingwithbeth.com	
Location	Boulder, Colorado	e.g. Palo Alto, CA

FIGURE 2.1 Update your profile settings by clicking on your username in the upper right corner of the Pinterest interface, then clicking on "Settings."

Using your business name can be a powerful way to spread the word about your brand to the Pinterest community. Because of the way Pinterest works, the names you enter in these fields will be repeated to other Pinterest users in a number of ways, including emails and various places within the platform's interface. Therefore, what you enter in these fields is worth careful consideration.

Whatever you choose, you'll want to make sure the words are readable and recognizable. This isn't a place to be clever or to use a name like "WriTeRgrl*222" as it will probably just confuse people! Include only alphabetical characters (not numbers) and make your name easy to understand. If you wouldn't want an email note going out to your followers with this name on it, then don't use it.

Pinterest does require you to put something in the "Last Name" box, so if you'd like to use your business name and your brand is more than one word, you can always divide up the name in the two fields. For example, "Joe's Shoe Repair" could enter "Joe's" in the "First Name" field, and "Shoe Repair" in the "Last Name" Field. Or you could add an asterisk in the Last Name Field, just to add a character and fulfill Pinterest's requirements. But you should be aware that the asterisk will show up on your profile and in Pinterest's auto-generated emails from you.

Unlike your username (which we'll discuss next), you don't have to have a unique profile name in Pinterest. For example, there are many Beth Haydens on Pinterest. You can use any profile name that makes sense for you and your business; just make sure to use both the first and the last name fields.

Username

Your username is a completely separate field from your Profile name in the Pinterest world. If you used Facebook to set up your Pinterest account, your username was automatically generated for you; however, if you used Twitter, you were asked to select a username during signup.

Your username does have to be unique because your Pinterest profile URL will be based on it. This means that you may need to use a number in your username (for example, "BethHayden23") in order to create one that's unique. Pinterest will tell you to choose a different username if the one you want is already taken.

Unless you have a major issue, I would advise that you don't try to change your username after you set up your account. If you do, you risk losing whatever followers you may already have. So if you get to choose your username, make sure to choose carefully!

About

The "About" field is a great way for you to tell the Pinterest world a little about who you are and what you'll be pinning about. It's a wonderful way to introduce others to your brand, so make sure not to waste this opportunity, and consider adding information like:

- What topics you'll be pinning about.

- Who you are trying to reach (your ideal client).

- Your Pinterest goals (e.g., starting discussion, educating users, entertaining, saving users' time and energy, etc.).

- Your website address. It won't be a live link, but it's not a bad idea to add it at the end of your "About" description. (You can drop the "http://" and just start the address with "www.")

Location

If you're a local business and would like other Pinterest users to know where you are based, then you should definitely add your location here. If you're a web-based business and would rather not (or don't need to) include your location, you can leave it blank.

Website

You can add a website URL to this field. Since your Pinterest profile supplies just one space to promote a website, carefully consider what you want to include in this field.

In most cases, you'll want to add a link to your main website. However, there might be instances where you want to consider adding a link to a special section of your site. This could be a unique store just for Pinterest users, or a landing page that offers a free report or special giveaway for followers who sign up for your mailing list.

We'll dive deeper into figuring out who you're trying to attract on Pinterest in our chapter on Pinterest strategy, which may impact what website you use in this field. For now, using your main website is fine. You'll be able to change the URL easily later if you want to make a switch.

Profile Image

Pinterest will automatically import your profile photo from your Twitter or Facebook account. If you would like to use a different photo, you can upload one in the "Image" section of your profile page. If you have a more recent photo on your Facebook or Twitter profile that you'd like Pinterest to use, just click on the "Refresh from Facebook/Twitter" button and Pinterest will check your social media profile for a new photo.

You might consider using a company logo as your Pinterest image in an effort to create brand awareness. It's fine to do that, too; just make sure that the logo includes the name of your business in a clear, easy-to-read font, so people will know who you are. For clarity's sake, it wouldn't hurt to create a version of your logo that is square shaped, so it will easily fit into the space Pinterest provides for your image. Otherwise, your logo may be cropped in a way that makes it difficult for your potential followers to read.

Facebook Options

Whether you created your account with Facebook or Twitter, you do have the option to link your Pinterest account to your personal Facebook timeline.

I was hesitant about doing this when I started using Pinterest because I was afraid that each one of my pins would be published individually to my Facebook timeline, and my friends would be buried under the huge volume of images and updates. But Pinterest actually manages this in a slick, efficient way. The site groups your pins so that they're published to your Facebook timeline as a set, instead of one at a time, so you needn't worry about overwhelming your friends.

It's a good idea to link your Pinterest account to your personal Facebook page as long as you are comfortable using your Facebook account for business purposes. If you're keeping your individual Facebook profile completely personal and you know you'll be using your Pinterest account to market your business, it might be a good idea to *not* link the two together. But feel free to link them if you're okay with mixing the two!

As of right now, Pinterest doesn't allow you to publish your pins automatically to your Facebook business page. However, that feature might be coming in the future.

Link to Twitter

When you created your account using your Twitter profile, the "Link to Twitter" option will be set to "On." Pinterest doesn't auto-publish anything when your profile is linked to Twitter in this way; however, this link does allow you to sync your profile photos and log in using your Twitter account, if you want.

Visibility

You will want your Pinterest profile to be findable in the search engines if you're using it for marketing purposes, so you want to set the "Hide Your Pinterest Profile from Search Engines" setting to "Off."

What's Next?

Once you've completed all your Pinterest profile updates, be sure to hit the big "Save Profile" button at the bottom of your profile screen.

Any time you need to tweak your settings—your profile image, website address, or social media preferences—you can always click on your profile name, then hit "Settings" to edit your Pinterest profile.

Now that you know how to set up a powerful Pinterest account and create a profile that will help you build your followers and drive traffic to your website, you're ready to begin the fun part: pinning!

Your Action Plan

- Decide whether you will create your Pinterest profile with your Facebook or Twitter account.

- Create your account and set up a powerful profile by filling in the About, Location, Website and other important fields with your critical business information.

- View your profile by clicking on your name (or business name) in the upper-right side of your screen, and view it with a critical eye. Did you miss anything? Will your initial profile make a good first impression on Pinterest users?

3

Before You Pin

Who Do You Want to Attract?

I'm about to say something some people might consider scandalous. Are you sitting down?

Here's the big shocker: If you don't think about strategy before you dive into Pinterest marketing, your pinning efforts are very likely to be a giant waste of time.

The first thing you need to do—even *before* you create your boards and pins—is to define your Pinterest strategy in order to determine which individuals you are trying to reach with your marketing efforts. And the more you know, the better your chances of being able to truly connect with those people. Defining your Pinterest strategy will also help you keep your focus where it needs to be: on bringing in leads and getting clients. And it will also help you recognize where Pinterest fits into your overall sales and marketing process.

In this chapter, I will help you define your ideal client, discuss how you can shape your content on Pinterest so it's highly attractive to that client, remind you of the purpose of social media promotion (including Pinterest marketing), and teach you the tools you need to make sure you don't get shunned from the Pinterest party for bad behavior.

Defining Your Ideal Client

Do you know who your ideal client is?

I'll bet that you currently have some customers you love to work with, people who energize and invigorate you. Think of one or two of your favorite clients, and consider what it is you enjoy about working with them. Why do you like helping that kind of person?

Author David Meerman Scott introduced the concept of "buyer personas" in his book, *The New Rules of Marketing and*

PR: How to use Social Media, Online Video, Mobile Applications, Blogs, News Releases and Viral Marketing to Reach Buyers Directly (now in it's third edition). Scott explains how creating a buyer persona (or ideal client) is one of the most important things your company can do before you begin publishing social media campaigns and reaching out via online tools.

Your buyer persona (or ideal client) is simply a descriptive profile of the kind of client you're trying to reach. Creating these kinds of profiles is a critical first step in defining your online strategy.

In *The New Rules of Marketing and PR*, Scott describes the following exercise, which one particular university conducted to define their buyer personas:

> *. . . if we break the buyers into distinct groups and then catalog everything we know about each one, we make it easier to create content targeted to each important demographic. For example, a college website usually has the goal of keeping alumni happy so that they donate money to their alma mater on a regular basis. A college might have two buyer personas for alumni: young alumni (those who graduated within the past 10 or 15 years) and older alumni. Universities also have a goal of recruiting students by driving them into the application process. The effective college site might have a buyer persona for the high school student who is considering college. But since the parents of the prospective student have very different informational needs, the site designers might build another buyer persona for parents. A college also has to keep its existing customers (current students) happy. In sum, that means a well-executed college site might target five distinct buyer personas. . . . By truly understanding the needs and the mindset of the five*

buyer personas, the college will be able to create appropriate content.

One of the best ways to create detailed, useful buyer persona profiles is to connect directly at the source; that is, to interview people. If you have direct access to some of your favorite clients, ask if you can talk to them on the phone for a few minutes.

You want to know as much as possible about each group of people, so ask as many questions as you can. How old are they? Do they have children? What specific problems do they wake up in the morning thinking about? What words do they use in describing themselves and the issues they are facing? What do they do for fun? What websites and social media tools do they use? What brings them joy?

Use the answers you gather to create a detailed profile on each type of client you are trying to attract to your business. Write the description of the profile down, add a photo, and hang it in a prominent place in your office as a reminder to everyone on your staff. You can even give each profile a nickname that helps you remember their preferences or distinctive traits, like "Sally the Bride-to-Be" or "John the Coach."

Oreck (@oreck), maker of vacuum cleaners, air purifiers, and other small appliances, focuses on women as their ideal clients. Oreck marketers could potentially create a detailed ideal-client profile called "Suzy Homemaker," and fill it in with details about where Suzy lives, whether she has kids or pets, and what her hobbies are. The U.S. Army (@usarmy) might have a few different profiles, including the young men and women they are looking to recruit, and members of the general public who are looking to support our troops.

This exercise may seem silly to you, but don't underestimate its importance. The more you know about the customers you're trying to reach on Pinterest, the more successful you'll be in connecting with them via your marketing efforts.

What Does Your Ideal Client Want?

Now that you've defined your ideal client and found out as much about him or her as you can, you have a much clearer position from which to start when you set up your Pinterest account.

Your pins and boards will be much more appealing to your target audience if you focus on your ideal client while you're pinning. Think about these various buyer personas when you're deciding whether or not to pin an image or video. Ask yourself, "Would my ideal client find this useful, educational, entertaining, or inspiring?" If the answer is yes, pin away! If not, keep looking for something that does fit into one of these categories.

The brand Pretzel Crisps (@PretzelCrisps) does a beautiful job of speaking to their ideal clients with their Pinterest boards. This smart snack company not only uses their pins to supply great ways to use their product (appetizers, dips, etc.), but, they have also loaded up their boards with other images and ideas that their followers and fans love. They even have a board called "Genius," which is filled with smart and clever ideas for homes and offices. Their content is appealing to the customers they're trying to reach because Pretzel Crisps knows exactly who they are looking to connect with.

Another example of a company that's using smart Pinterest strategy is the AARP (@AARP_Official). Although this membership association is new to Pinterest, they've already got a good start—they have cleverly-named boards that reach out to their target audience of seniors, like "50+ Technology" and "Movies for Grownups." Senior members on Pinterest know that this content is just for them, because it's personalized specifically for the needs and desires of the 50+ crowd. And when customers know that you've taken the time to figure out precisely what they want, they'll keep coming back for more!

Pinterest: One Piece of Your Overall Marketing Strategy

It's easy to get lost in the circus of social media. Between Facebook, Twitter, LinkedIn, Google+, and Pinterest, we often trick ourselves into believing that we're being incredibly productive by spending 10 hours a day interacting with people via all these different platforms. To complicate things even further, it seems like a new social media tool arrives on the scene every six months, and the social media gurus start yelling that you *must have a presence* within this newest site—otherwise, your business is completely sunk.

Sit back, take a deep breath, and let the circus music fade away. I'm going to straighten out some misconceptions for you.

When it comes to online marketing, your goals are simple: Drive traffic back to your website, add people to your mailing list, and turn those visitors into buyers.

Picture your marketing strategy as the wheel of a bicycle. Your content-rich website or blog is the hub of that wheel, and social media tools like Facebook, Twitter, and Pinterest are the spokes. And while they are very *important* spokes, they are nonetheless merely spokes. Social media tools should act as distribution and traffic-building mechanisms for your website's top-quality content. Building relationships and trust on social media is incredibly important, as well. However, if the people with whom you're building these connections never leave your Pinterest profile or Facebook page, then you are spinning your wheels (and probably wasting a lot of time).

Pinterest is no different than any other social media site. If your Pinterest efforts are not helping you bring people to your business's door, you need to change the way you are using the site.

We'll talk later in this book (Chapter 10) about ways to track Pinterest traffic, sign-ups, and conversions, so you know which of your efforts are working (and which are not). But for now, remember this: Your goal is to increase the number of leads your company acquires and the number of sales you close. Period.

We all need to remember that participating in social media circles is *a means to an end*—not the end itself.

So remember what your goals are before you go further in this process. You might even post those goals somewhere you'll see them often (e.g., on your computer screen, above your desk) so that your Pinterest efforts aren't in vain. Building relationships is great—but you want to do so in a way that helps you meet your larger objectives.

Let Your Personality Shine

Before you start pinning—in fact, before you even create your account—you and your staff should also think about things that you are passionate about that you can use as springboards for remarkable content. The word "interest" is built right into Pinterest's brand name, so don't commit the cardinal sin of being boring when you pin.

Bethany Salvon (@beersandbeans) of the beautiful travel blog BeersandBeans.com lets her brand's personality shine through on her Pinterest profile. Some of her boards are typical of what you would expect from a travel blogger, including one called "The Wander Wall," which is a group of photos, advice, tips, and personal stories curated by several of the world's best full-time travel bloggers. Salvon also has collections on quirkier topics, like her "VW and Tiny Homes" board, which is dedicated to minimalist living spaces such as Volkswagen buses and itty-bitty homes. It's a beautiful and unique board, and it completely fits with the BeersandBeans.com brand—but it's remarkable and sticky. People will remember it later, pass it on via social media, and be able to connect with Salvon through this quirky content.

Also remember that you can use images and videos to promote the *idea* behind your brand when you're figuring out how to reach your ideal client through Pinterest. What does your company stand for? What are its values and principles? What kind of lifestyle does it try to promote, and why does that lifestyle appeal to your ideal client?

BlogFrog, a traffic- and community-building tool for bloggers, has a great Pinterest strategy that spotlights their adorable mascot, the frog. The BlogFrog team pins images and videos that appeal to their primary audience—women bloggers. They even curate a BlogFrog Fashion board. The board isn't just a generic fashion board, however; it highlights clothing and accessories in BlogFrog's signature color (green, of course). The images are fun and cute, and BlogFrog manages to walk the very narrow line between under-promoting (not mentioning the brand or products at all) and over-promoting (jamming the brand down people's throats at every opportunity). BlogFrog's Pinterest campaigns strike a perfect balance.

If you pin things that you feel passionate about and that showcase your personality, your enthusiasm will be contagious— and you will create compelling content that your followers will love.

Becoming a Source of Valuable Information

The pinners behind Chobani yogurt's Pinterest boards are smart cookies. The brand knows that merely pinning images from their own site isn't the best use of their Pinterest presence. So instead, they create insightful boards and pins that they know their ideal clients will love.

Chobani (@chobani) maintains several different boards that feature a variety of recipes from many different websites and blogs. And while many of the recipes include yogurt as one of the ingredients, not all of them do. The yogurt company knows that their target audience (women, who do most of the grocery shopping) are always on the lookout for delicious and simple recipes to feed their hungry hoards at home. So instead of just pinning links from the Chobani website, they're in the business of solving problems for their followers. Chobani also gets the opportunity to educate the public about their products, but that isn't the main reason the yogurt company pins recipes.

In short, Chobani shares information and solves problems, without overtly *selling*.

Here's an important news flash: No one actually cares about your products and services in and of themselves. People want to solve their problems, and that's what they need or want your products and services for. Pinterest gives you the incredible opportunity to become a valued source of information to the folks you're trying to reach. And if you *view yourself as a source of information and ideas*, rather than someone hawking your wares, you will be far more successful on Pinterest than if you focus only on promoting and pinning your own products and services.

Ann Handley and C.C. Chapman, authors of the book *Content Rules: How to Create Killer Blogs, Podcasts, Videos, Ebooks, Webinars (and More) that Engage Customers and Ignite Your Business*, advise becoming a source of valuable information online:

> *Good content shares or solves; it doesn't shill. In other words, it doesn't hawk your wares or push sales-driven messages. Rather, it creates value by positioning you as a reliable and valuable source of vendor-agnostic information . . .* [the content you share] *is of high value to your customers, in whatever way resonates best with them.*

Sharing great content is always welcome on social media sites, including Pinterest. Over-promotion and narcissism are not.

■ ■ ■

As you practice pinning for your ideal client and expressing your brand's personality through Pinterest's tools, your instincts about what kind of content to publish will get better and better, and your following will grow. And when you know how your Pinterest efforts fit in with the rest of your online marketing strategy, the various sites where you have a social media presence will work together like a finely tuned machine.

Now that you're clear on your marketing goals and strategy on Pinterest, let's move on to the really fun stuff: learning how to pin!

Your Action Plan

- Create your ideal client profile(s).

- Brainstorm the needs and wants of your ideal client(s).

- Make a list of ways that you can solve or share on Pinterest, to help out your ideal client.

- Regularly remind yourself that social media is a means to end—not an end in and of itself.

The Basics of Pinning

Beautiful Boards and Compelling Pins

According to their website, Pinterest's mission is "to connect everyone in the world through the 'things' they find interesting. We think that a favorite book, toy, or recipe can reveal a common link between two people. With millions of new pins added every week, Pinterest is connecting people all over the world based on shared tastes and interests." The main tools that Pinterest uses to make connections between people are pins and pinboards.

Your company can also use pins to facilitate connections, build community, and attract your perfect clients. And Pinterest's simple user interface makes it really easy to do that.

When using Pinterest, you will place images, or *pins*, into pinboards (groups of pins) on different topics. This chapter will cover the different methods you can use to pin images, as well as some guidelines for creating compelling content that will attract lots of followers.

Boards

Pinboards, or *boards*, as they are known in the Pinterest world, are the virtual bulletin boards you use to group the images that you find interesting or compelling. For example, some of my boards include: "Blogging and Social Media Tips," "Pinterest is Great for Your Biz," "Writers and Writing," "Killer Marketing Advice," "I Believe," and "Amusing." Most of the pins I collect every day go into one of these boards. I also have boards for entertaining, decorating, handy ideas, and travel.

Vacuum cleaner company Oreck (@oreck) maintains a board called "Clean Made Easy," which spotlights smart ways to clean your home, including methods to wash your glass cooktop, living room baseboards, and gold jewelry. The tagline on

Oreck's website is also "Clean Made Easy"—making the naming of this board particularly clever and useful from a branding perspective.

Naming Your Boards

You will need to come up with a unique name for each board that you create. It's likely that your instinct when you get started, like that of many Pinterest beginners, will be to create broadly-themed boards that allow you to pin lots of images under a single topic. However, I must issue a warning: *Fight the urge to do this*.

Yes, it seems like it would be an easy way to gather many different images in one place. However, you want your board topics and names to be *as specific as possible*. For example, I would advise a travel company against creating a board with the general name "Cruises" in favor of the much more specific and memorable title *Fun Family Caribbean Cruises*. The difference may seem subtle, but as many business owners know—it's a critical one. Your customers have varied preferences in terms of the products and services they use. Which of these boards are you more likely to forward to a friend who is considering taking her family on a cruise to Aruba?

It's also a good idea to keep your board names short, snappy, and to the point. When someone clicks on your Pinterest account to view your boards and decide whether or not they want to follow you, you want your board names to look unique and compelling to them.

The latest version of Pinterest profiles (as of March 2012) gives users a snapshot view of a member's boards upon viewing their profile. However, the disadvantage of this new view is that long board names can cut off on this profile page. Therefore, the meanings of clever names can get lost in translation. This is yet another reason to keep your board names to five or six words at most, and to check to make sure your board's name doesn't get cut off on your profile page.

The Travel Channel (@travelchannel) has mastered the art of creating short and compelling board titles, with boards like "Travel Bucket List" and "Festivals and Events." Travel writer Jodi Ettenberg (@jodiettenberg) also has short, compelling board titles, including "food, glorious food" and "trees that look like broccoli" (see Figure 4.1). Yes, she actually has a board named that—doesn't it pique your curiosity and make you want to check it out?

Each pinboard has its own unique URL. For example, the URL for one of my most popular boards, called "Pinterest is Great for Your Biz," is at this location: www.pinterest.com/bethhayden/pinterest-is-great-for-your-biz.

You can share this board on your website, via email, or on Facebook, Twitter, or any other social media outlet. All you have to do is copy and paste the board name to give people a direct hyperlink back to that collection of pins.

A word of warning here: If you go back later and change your board name, Pinterest will change the board's URL. So if you link to that board from Facebook, Twitter, your personal or

FIGURE 4.1 Jodi Ettenberg (@jodiettenberg) uses short, quirky, memorable board names.

company website, or anywhere else, you will need to update the link.

One last word about boards: Pinterest lets you choose a cover image for each board, which will be viewable from your profile page. You can access your profile page by clicking on your account name in the upper right of your screen on your Pinterest home page. Then hover over any of the boards on your profile, and you'll see a button called "Edit Board Cover." When you click on that button, Pinterest lets you select an image to use as that board's cover photo. Make sure to choose clear, easy-to-understand images as your board covers to entice people to check out those boards!

How to Pin

We've discussed how Pinterest allows users to create theme-based image collections called boards. Each of the images in your collections is called a pin, which is simply a piece of content that you have added to one of your boards. In most cases, each pin links back to a website that gives more information about that image.

There are three ways to pin an image to one of your boards:

1. Using the Pin It bookmarklet.

2. Copying and pasting a link to an image.

3. Uploading your own image.

Let's look at each one in detail.

Method One: The Pin It Bookmarklet

By far the easiest way to pin an image is to use the Pin It bookmarklet, which will install a "Pin It" button to a toolbar in your browser.

If you haven't already done so, install the Pin It bookmarklet by going to www.pinterest.com/about/goodies.

Once you've installed the bookmarklet, you can pin an image from any web page. If you're on a web page or blog post and want to pin an image from that page, click on your Pin It bookmarklet button. Pinterest will bring up a pop-up box that lets you choose which image or video you'd like to pin from that page, then ask you what board and description you want to use. (A description for each pin is required.) Pinterest will then automatically grab the link for the pin, so the pin will link to that page when it is added to your board.

Here's a slick time-saving tip: The bookmarklet can quickly auto-fill a pin description for you, too. Before clicking the "Pin It" button in your bookmark bar, highlight some text (like the blog post title or a juicy paragraph from an article) from the page you are going to pin from. Then click the "Pin It" button. Your highlighted text will automatically become the pin's description. This saves a lot of time when you're pinning quickly and don't feel like being creative with your descriptions.

Method Two: The Add-a-Pin Method

You can pin images from websites even if you don't want to use the bookmarklet—or if it doesn't work with your browser. Just click on the "Add +" button in the navigation area of your Pinterest homepage, then select "Add a Pin" to manually add the URL of the web page from which you'd like to pin an image (see Figure 4.2). A pop-up box will appear. Add your URL, and click on "Find Images." Pinterest will then search that page for pinnable images.

It's worth noting that, in my experience, the Add-a-Pin manual method doesn't find pinnable images nearly as well as the bookmarklet does. This is why I recommend using the bookmarklet method if possible.

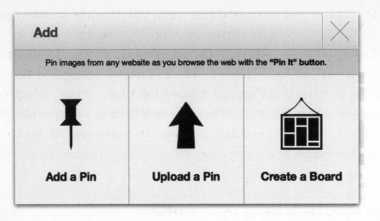

FIGURE 4.2   Use the "Add" button in Pinterest to upload images or manually add pins from websites.

Method Three: The Upload-a-Pin Method

You can use this method to upload your own images to Pinterest. Simply click on the "Add +" button in the navigation area of your Pinterest homepage, then click on "Upload a Pin." Browse to find the image you'd like to upload, select it, and click on "Open" to upload it. Then select a board to pin your uploaded image to, write a short description, and click on "Pin It."

If you would like to add a URL to your images later, you can do that, too. Just click on the pin, then click the "Edit" button that appears in the upper left corner of the image when you hover over the picture. Then edit the "Link" field in the pin settings to route the pin to a blog post on your website, a landing page, or anywhere else you want to link to on the web. Please keep in mind, however, that you should try to retain links to other people's artwork, photos, etc. so that the pins still link to the image's original source. Please see Chapter 14 for more information on ethical pinning.

Repinning

It's also possible to repin other people's pins on Pinterest, much the same way that you can retweet something in the Twitter world. You repin someone else's pin when you like that pin and would like to use that image on one of your own boards.

To do so, just click on a pin to open up a larger version of it, then click on the image to make sure the image links to its original source (we'll go into more detail on this in Chapter 14) then click on "Repin" in the upper-left area of the pin. Select which one of your boards you'd like to repin the image to, then click on "Pin It."

Adding Compelling Descriptions

Each time you pin an image, you will need to add a description to it. This is something you want to consider carefully, since a compelling description has the potential to make a huge difference in whether or not your image is shared in the Pinterest community. Since you want your image to get shared, because it helps you get more followers, you'll want to write great descriptions!

Pinterest gives you up to 500 characters to use in the description field. Your description can be one line or one phrase, if that's all you need to properly label your image; or, you might need to make it several paragraphs long. A general rule of thumb is that you should use the exact number of characters you need to properly describe your image and give your followers some context—and not one character more. Long descriptions just for the sake of writing more words won't work in your favor, but if you need several paragraphs to properly describe the image, go ahead and use them.

Examples of good descriptions:

- **For an image of several cameras that links to a photography site:** "Keep your camera lenses in tip-top shape with these cleaning tips."

- **For a link to a how-to Flickr article:** "I have been looking for something exactly like this for my clients. It's called

'A Complete Guide to Finding and Using Incredible Flickr Images.' Excellent info here for bloggers looking for photos to add to blog posts."

Clearly, these descriptions are much more powerful and explanatory than "Wow" or "This is great."

Always make sure that your description matches the content of the pin and the link that it sends users to. Don't pull a bait-and-switch and try to entice people to click on your pin under false pretense. Honesty in Pinterest—as in all other areas of business—is always the best policy.

I definitely recommend that you show some personality in writing your descriptions. Unfortunately, I've found many descriptions to be incredibly dull, because pinners don't take the time to fully flesh them out. You want to write a story, add a note about why you're excited about the pin, or infuse the description with some character. Figure 4.3 shows my top-performing pin and its accompanying description.

Additionally, don't be afraid to reveal some things about yourself. You can admit, for example, that you covet something, have a secret guilty pleasure, or that you're not as organized as you like to be. Your followers, as well as current and potential customers, will admire your honesty—and probably feel that they have something in common with you! You should speak as an individual, too-. While you may have your staff members pinning as a team, it's important to let them all know that they can be themselves on Pinterest. After all, we do business with people we like, and it's a lot easier to like someone when they can let their hair down a little.

The ideal trifecta that you're seeking in social media relationships is to get your potential clients to know, like, and trust you. If you can give people the opportunity to get to know you, start to like you, and begin to trust you through your content and relationship-building efforts, you've built a solid foundation for them to become incredibly loyal customers. Pinning gives

They're STICKERS! How cool is this??

FIGURE 4.3 My (very surprising) best-performing pin, to date. Note the enthusiastic description! This pin currently has over 600 repins.

Source: Image courtesy of Trading Phrases, www.tradingphrases.com.

you a great way to build relationships with people to do all three of these important steps!

Check out Chapters 6 and 11 for more suggestions and guidelines about the kinds of useful and interesting content you can pin that will help you build a fanatical following on Pinterest!

■ ■ ■

Now that you know the basics of pinning and how to create interesting content that your followers will love, let's talk about some basic ways to begin interacting with other Pinterest users in genuine, authentic ways.

Your Action Plan

- Install the Pin It bookmarklet on your favorite browser.

- Create some initial pinboards with creative and interesting titles.

- Start adding some pins and practice writing compelling descriptions.

Connecting with Pinterest Users

Commenting, Tagging, Liking, and Hashtags

Now that you've set up your profile and have started pinning some images and organizing your boards, you want to start building your Pinterest community. People who follow your profile or your individual boards in the Pinterest world are called (appropriately) *followers*.

Just like Facebook friends and fans and Twitter followers, your Pinterest followers are valuable. And one of the best ways to attract them is to effectively use Pinterest's built-in connection tools.

We'll talk in more detail about how to nurture relationships with your followers in Chapter 8. For now, let's look at the four main ways that Pinterest users interact with each other.

Commenting

Commenting in Pinterest works exactly the same way as it does in Facebook. You can leave a short reply under any user's pin (or one of your own). Just click on the field under the pin that says, "Add a comment," type your reply, and click on "Post Reply."

When commenting, make sure you are adding something valuable to the conversation because a pin *is* the start of a conversation! (See Figure 5.1.) Whether you are the first commenter or the seventy-first, make sure you're adding something interesting or useful to the discussion. Give an example, agree with the person's point, disagree respectfully, or tell the person why you like their pin or board.

The best analogy to keep in mind as you are commenting is that you're like someone who's joining a cocktail party. You wouldn't interrupt a group of people talking just to give them a pushy sales offer; in the same way, you shouldn't interrupt a conversation on Pinterest just to pitch your products and

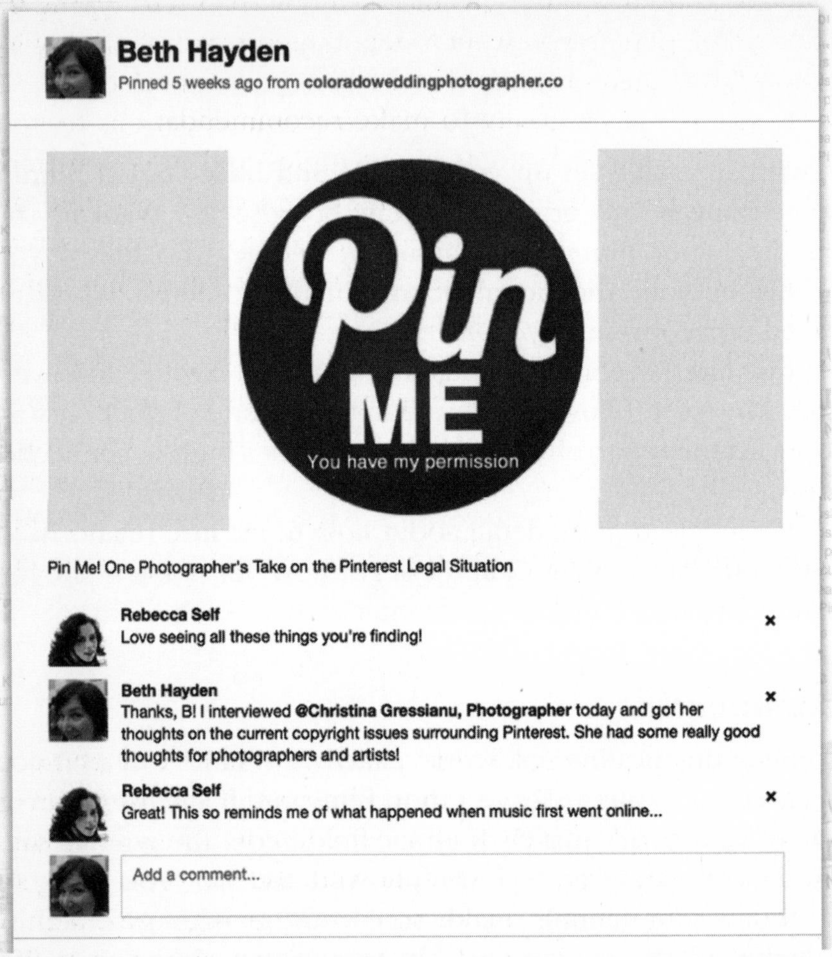

Beth Hayden
Pinned 5 weeks ago from **coloradoweddingphotographer.co**

Pin Me! One Photographer's Take on the Pinterest Legal Situation

Rebecca Self   ×
Love seeing all these things you're finding!

Beth Hayden   ×
Thanks, B! I interviewed **@Christina Gressianu, Photographer** today and got her
thoughts on the current copyright issues surrounding Pinterest. She had some really good
thoughts for photographers and artists!

Rebecca Self   ×
Great! This so reminds me of what happened when music first went online...

Add a comment...

FIGURE 5.1 A Pinterest discussion in the comments area. Note that I tagged @Christina Gressianu (@photocg) in the comments.

services. Just as it is on other social media sites—and in most marketing nowadays—over-promotion is frowned upon on Pinterest.

Tagging

You can tag other Pinterest users in your comments if you'd like to mention them or recommend a particular pin to them.

The way to do this is to type an @ symbol, then start typing the name of the person you want to tag. Pinterest will then provide a drop-down menu of users from which you can select.

Tagging is a great way to make recommendations to your current and potential clients about topics and pins you think they would enjoy. You can also ask them questions, find out about their experiences with your products, or just discover more about them and the kind of Pinterest content they enjoy. Remember that the goal is to build relationships with people, so use tagging strategically. Don't be a pest!

You'll receive an email when someone tags you in a Pinterest comment. This means that whoever wrote the comment wants to draw you into the conversation in some way; some people take it as an opportunity to connect with that person. So if you been tagged, find out if that user has a question or comment, and then reply to them!

Liking

Just as you can "Like" a status update, comment, or photo in Facebook, you can "Like" a pin in Pinterest. It's a quick way of giving someone a thumbs-up for her content. When you Like a pin, you don't post it to your followers the way you do when you repin something; instead, you're just giving a little sign of approval. To Like a pin, just hover over that pin on your Pinterest home page, and you'll see a Like button appear. Click on that button to give your approval!

You can feel free to use Likes generously—they're a great way to connect with other users. Pinterest also keeps track of all your Likes; you can see them by clicking "Likes" on your Pinterest home page (it's under your profile name). This feature allows you to go back and revisit pins you've Liked. This can be helpful if you later want to comment on a pin you've Liked, or embed the pin in a blog post. (We'll talk in detail about how to embed pins in your blog posts in Chapter 9.)

I published a guest post on Copyblogger called "56 Ways to Promote Your Business on Pinterest," in February of 2012, and the article got pinned like crazy. I Liked as many of those pins as I could, then commented on the pin to thank the pinner for their interest. I gained a lot of new followers this way, and found some great new pinners to follow, too!

Hashtags

Hashtags are used to categorize messages in Pinterest comments and descriptions. You simply put the # symbol right in front of keywords or topics in your comments without leaving a space between the # and the word, or between the words themselves, as shown in Figure 5.2. Tagging helps people find your pins and boards. Some popular hashtags from Pinterest include #infographics, #wedding, and #recipes. You can come up with your own hashtag, or use ones that you see in Pinterest.

When you use a hashtag, the # sign and the word following it become a link on which users can click to get to similar pins.

56 Ways to Market Your Business on Pinterest #pinterestmarketing

 Add a comment...

FIGURE 5.2 A Pinterest hashtag. The term @pinterestmarketing is clickable.

When you click on #recipes, for instance, users will be taken to a page of current recipes in Pinterest (with the most current ones at the top of the page).

As Pinterest grows, I believe they will expand their usage of hashtags, and make their search function better. For now, you can use hashtags to denote the general topic of your pin and to find other similar pins.

Connecting with Your Ideal Client

We talked in Chapter 3 about creating an ideal client profile that helps shape your Pinterest strategy. One of the keys to using Pinterest's connection tools is to remember that your ideal client is an individual who is using social media because he or she likes to be *social*.

You want to use comments, tagging, likes, and hashtags in the spirit of building a relationship with that individual. Nothing makes a company more human—and therefore more appealing—than seeing its staffers engage in genuine, warm, one-on-one interaction (whether in person or on social media). And that is exactly what these techniques give you the opportunity to do!

Your Action Plan

- Jump into the conversation on Pinterest by commenting on users' boards.

- "Like" some pins that you enjoyed or learned something from.

- In a comment, tag a user who you think would enjoy a particular pin.

- Use hashtags to link your pins with other similar ones.

Part Two

Pinning for Profits

6

The Power of Pictures

How to Create Compelling Visual
Business Content

Therapist Tamara Suttle, LPC, (@tamaragsuttle) had a problem. She works with new therapists, many of them completely inexperienced, and she wanted to show them ways to create a warm, welcoming therapist's office. Many of these therapists are just getting started in establishing their practices, and have never had to set up a therapist's office before—some have never even set foot in one!

"You need to think about the impact your office has on your clients," Suttle told them. "It's a very important first impression." But while the terms "warm" and "inviting" are easy to say, they are much more difficult to pull off in terms of designing the environment in a real-life office setting. And it's hard to find the words to describe what a "welcoming office" looks like. So when Suttle started using Pinterest, she saw an incredible opportunity.

She started pinning resources about waiting rooms and office spaces, and quickly amassed a large collection of ideas and suggestions about the topic on her "Private Practice from the Inside Out" board. She's used that board to pin everything from flavored water recipes (courtesy of celebrity chef Jamie Oliver) to example images of actual therapists' offices. It's a veritable smorgasbord of inspiration for therapists who are seeking ways to set up their very first therapeutic space. And Suttle communicates her expert advice beautifully through the power of pictures.

Oreck (@oreck) has a specific and effective strategy for using visual content on Pinterest:

Our content strategy is simple: pin things that our customer would find interesting. Much of the time, we are able to relate this back to Oreck, our products or our values. We have a board for each of our newest products (vacuums, air purifiers and steam mops), but it only includes photos of the products in use in real people's homes, mostly from the bloggers we work with as a part of our blogger outreach program.

We don't want to be like many other brands that pin all product shots. That's why we have boards like "Furry Friends" [featuring photos of loveable pets] *and "Stunning Floors"* [showing beautiful home flooring options]. *We even have a board that's completely dedicated to* [our "signature"] *color blue . . . as it's fun to look at.*

We want to connect with our customer through her pets, her unique floor surfaces, or a favorite color and remind her of the solutions Oreck products can provide to meet the needs in her home and make her life just a little bit easier.

Tamara Suttle and Oreck have mastered the art of leveraging the power of pictures. They are both purveyors of interesting, compelling content on Pinterest, and have embraced the role of being content providers for their followers.

What to Think about When Publishing Pinterest Content

When you use social media sites like Facebook, Twitter, and Pinterest, you must embrace the role of being a content marketer. Copyblogger.com (one of the largest and most successful social media blogs on the web) explains this role as follows:

Content Marketing *means creating and freely sharing informative content as a means of converting prospects into customers and customers into repeat buyers . . . repeated and regular exposure* [to content] *builds a* *relevant relationship that provides multiple opportunities for conversion, rather than a "one-shot" all-or-nothing sales approach.*[1]

As a smart marketer, you share content via your website, your Twitter feed, and your YouTube channel. Your platform on Pinterest is just another extension of that content marketing system; the only difference is that all the content is visual (images and videos). The underlying principles of content marketing are exactly the same.

To market well using social media sites, you need to make sure that every piece of content you publish either solves a problem for your audiences, or entertains them—preferably both. This principle of "Share or Solve; Don't Shill," as *Content Rules* authors Ann Handley and C.C. Chapman call it, is critical to successful online marketing. Once you establish good rapport with your audience through the fantastic content you publish on your website (and other social media platforms), they will buy from you because they like and trust you. But if you skip over the crucially important step of publishing good content—and only distribute fluff or sales messages—your audience won't trust you, and your web traffic and social media interactions will never convert to customers and clients.

One thing that may help you when you're considering publishing a piece of content on Pinterest is to ask yourself how you want people to *feel* after they see a particular image or video. Because visual content can be truly compelling and emotional, you can actually evoke certain feelings in your audience—preferably positive ones like joy, delight, satisfaction, or curiosity. So ask yourself how you want your audience to feel, then ask if your image or video contributes to that feeling. If it does, great; you've got a winner! If not, put the mouse

---

[1] www.copyblogger.com/content-marketing.

down and reconsider. This is a good way to evaluate not only individual pins on Pinterest, but pinboards, too.

Consider as well whether your content is evergreen. Does it have staying power; will it still be compelling and interesting if a user sees it a year—or five years—from today? *Evergreen content* never goes out of date, and it is relevant to Pinterest followers year after year. You want to have a mix of timely, current images and evergreen content that will stay fresh year after year.

Ways to Publish Content

You have a few options for sources of images and videos for your boards when publishing content on Pinterest:

1. Repinning great content from other Pinterest users.

2. Pinning your own unique content from other sources (other websites, blogs, etc.).

3. Creating your own unique Pinterest content.

All three of these options can contribute greatly to your content. However, the brands and businesses that do the best on Pinterest are usually those that have the most original content; that is, images that are not repinned from another Pinterest user.

I have noticed that my most popular content—that which other users repin and comment on most often—is my original content. The images that go viral on Pinterest are the original things I find from other places (or create myself). Of course, you must test out what works for your audience. (Check out Chapter 10 for more information on learning what works for your audience.) However, it truly seems that one of the best ways for most businesses to stand out is to pin something brand new and original.

Statistics says that over 80 percent of Pinterest content is repinned from somewhere else in the Pinterest world, which means that you see a lot of recycled images. If you're already a Pinterest user, you've probably had the experience that I've had: You keep seeing the same bunny picture, outfit, or celebrity glam shot, over and over again on your Pinterest page as that image makes its way around Pinterest and continually gets repinned.

Compare the experience of seeing this same old picture again and again with that of seeing a *brand new image* that no one else has pinned—perhaps something that is so unique you've never seen anything like it. It's no secret that people love novelty and originality, and discovering new things. So remember that finding unique images to pin is a critical component of Pinterest success.

■ ■ ■

Think of your responsibilities as a Pinterest publisher as twofold:

1. You need to be a **curator of great content** from all over the web (cherry-picking the best information from Pinterest and the wider web world of your followers); and

2. You also want to **publish original content** in the form of awesome photos, videos, and other types of images.

In Chapter 8, "The Care and Feeding of Pinterest Followers," we'll cover more detailed information on being the best content curator you can possibly be, so you can cultivate loyalty from your followers. For now, however, we'll use the next section to focus on the second half of the Pinterest publishing equation: creating your own high-quality content to share on your pinboards. I'll give you the tools and tips you need to create visual content that is so compelling that you may not even need to distribute it yourself; your readers, fans, and followers will do it for you!

Guidelines for great pinning are as follows:

• Your images should be beautiful, remarkable, and interesting.

• You want to post pictures that are attractive and well lit. If you plan to upload or pin a lot of your own photography, this is good time to invest in a great quality digital SLR camera. Remember that good-quality photography will get more attention on Pinterest.

- Don't make your images too tall and skinny, or pin anything that is over 5,000 pixels tall. This is crucial because the "Repin" and "Like" buttons are at the top of each pin. If a user has to scroll a long way just to see the entire image, then it's very unlikely they will scroll back up to repin your image.

- Remember to caption the great images you create with keyword-rich descriptions so that people can easily find them when they search. Keyword-rich means that you want to use terms that are specific and meaningful to your potential customers. For example, instead of a caption saying, "Our lovely spring bouquet," use some specific words and say something like, "Our lovely spring bouquet of *white hydrangea* and *pink roses*."

Here are some ideas for creating interesting, highly pinnable images that pinners will love to share:

- **Behind-the-scenes images of your office, your staff, and your business processes.** Take photos of your offices, factories, or other company buildings, and show your followers a behind-the-scenes view of how you make things—and even ways in which *you* use your own products and services.

- **Photo badges.** Consider making pin-friendly photo banners for your blog post and web pages. To do so, just take an attractive, clear photo—hopefully one that has a bit of open area where you can add some text and have it remain readable—and then use a photo-editing tool to add a title to the photo (see the "Tools" section at the end of this chapter for suggestions on photo editors). When they're done well, photo badges are exceptionally effective on Pinterest. Consider using the blog post title (if it's interesting and attention-grabbing) or whatever you would normally put in the description field, and just add that text directly to your image. Make sure the text is large enough that it's easily readable when it's been pinned. See Figure 6.1 for an example of a highly effective photo badge used by blogger Nester Smith.

- **Geographic images of the city or town where your office is based.** BlogFrog (@blogfrog) maintains a board all about Boulder, Colorado, the location of their main office. It shows a lot of personality and helps people get to know their company better. Try this with your own company hometown, even if that city or town is far off the beaten path; in

FIGURE 6.1 One of Nester Smith's (www.thenester.com, @nesters) very popular photo pins.

fact, the fewer people who know about it, the more interesting and unique your information will be.

- **Event photos.** Make a commitment to taking good, clear, crisp photos at your company events and then sharing them on Pinterest. This is a great way to let your customers (and potential clients) get a glimpse into how your company works, and it's also a great way to impart real, useful information. It's great for employee morale, too!

- **Mindmaps.** People love mindmaps because they provide a visual representation of ideas, how those ideas connect together, and how they're organized. It's like seeing an image of what a brainstorming session looks like. Mindmaps have a very high perceived value because of our insatiable need for new ideas—leverage this perception by experimenting with using mindmaps as content on your blog posts and directly to Pinterest.

- **Infographics.** Infographics are graphic visual representations of information or data. They're very hot right now, and they can be very successful on Pinterest. Since infographics have the natural tendency to be long and tall, they can be a little harder to share on Pinterest; many are well over 5,000 pixels tall. So you may want to consider creating a smaller graphic that represents your infographic, then linking that smaller image to the full infographic.

- **Ebook/book covers.** If your company has a stockpile of ebook covers (free or paid) that you can share, these also make great Pinterest content. And if you're an author, you should *absolutely* pin your book covers! If your book has sold internationally, you can pin the global covers, too, so people can see what the book looks like in different languages.

- **Slides.** If your company event, presentation, or class also includes a slide-show presentation, save one of the slides as an image file, then share it on Pinterest, too. You could create a "Workshops" board; if your company does several different kinds of workshops, you could have a board for each type.

- **Videos.** If you maintain a YouTube channel or have other useful and interesting video content floating around, pin it! Videos make great Pinterest content. You can pin workshops or classes, client testimonials, and promotional videos. Picture your Pinterest account as an offshoot video channel, similar to YouTube. Blendtec (@blendtec), a company that makes high-quality blenders, has a Pinterest video board dedicated to recipes for soups, sauces, smoothies, and other blender-friendly fare.

Here are some tools that can help you create great images and video content:

- **PicMonkey** (www.picmonkey.com). This is an easy tool for creating beautiful photo badges and other pin-friendly images. The following is a link to a video that teaches you how to make a pin-worthy photo badge using PicMonkey: www.youtu.be/L_RqRRgwKTQ.

- **Share As Image** (www.shareasimage.com). This service is a brilliant fix for a common problem. What do you do when the blog post or web page you want to pin doesn't include a pinnable image or video? You highlight the text you'd like to pin, click on this button in your browser, and ShareAsImage will create a nice-looking badge with your quote text in it. Buying the Pro version of ShareAsImage gives you more options for changing the colors and fonts of your badges.

- **Mindmapping tools.** While iMindMap is my favorite mindmapping tool, XMind and MindMeister are also great choices. Look for software that is easy to work with and that fits with your natural process of brainstorming and organizing content. And make sure you pick a tool that lets you export your final mindmap as a .jpeg or other image file, so you can easily use it in a blog post or upload it to a Pinterest board.

- **Screenflow (Mac) and Camtasia (PC).** These tools are my favorite screencasting tools. They let you create videos on your computer by recording what you're doing on your computer screen while you provide a voiceover description. Great for software how-to videos and other similar content.

- **Hipstamatic app for iPhone.** This app lets you create all kinds of cool effects with your iPhone photos. From what I hear, it can make *anything* look cooler. Try it out if you use your iPhone frequently for pictures.

- **Infographics.** If you're interested in doing infographics for your company, I recommend working with a design firm who specializes in this area. If you see infographics that you really love on the web, find out who created them. And when you're working with a design firm to create images like this, make sure you're really clear about what you need from their design work and who your intended audience is.

Your Action Plan

- Start building your Pinterest content library with event photos, slideshows, photo badges, and so forth. Remember to make your content clear, interesting, and compelling. Good-quality photos are a must.

- Download or research some of the tools listed at the end of this chapter to help you create great content.

- Start a YouTube channel (if you don't already have one) for sharing company videos, and create a video board on your Pinterest account.

Getting Shared

How to Optimize Your Website for Pinners

As Pinterest continues to grow, you can bet there will be an increasing number of pinners cruising the web, looking for great content to add to their boards. This chapter will teach you how to optimize your blog posts and web pages so that Pinterest users will feel right at home pinning your content.

Remember that the more people pin your content, the more traffic you'll get to your website. Therefore, you'll want to make every effort to roll out the welcome mat for pinners. Here are some easy steps you can take to optimize your website or blog for Pinterest.

Adding Images to Your Website Content

The very first thing you should do to make your website more Pinterest-user-friendly is include an image (or several) in every single blog post and page you publish. If you publish a blog post without an image, it won't get shared on Pinterest—it's that simple. Visual content is *everything* with pinners! So if you start to get lazy about adding images, remember that not using an image in your post means no one will pin it.

Keep in mind that the more beautiful, interesting, or compelling an image is, the more it will get pinned. The images that appeal to Pinterest members are powerful, emotive, and fun, which is something to remember when you choose your pictures. The good news is that interesting images also work wonders for your regular blog readers, so putting photos in your blog posts will be great for your blog traffic, too. All those types of powerful visual content discussed in Chapter 6—staff photos, behind-the-scenes videos, mindmaps, and so forth—are all examples of great images for blog posts.

I'm also a big fan of buying stock photography for your blog posts and web pages. There are several stock photo sites from which you can purchase beautiful images, and acquire royalty-free licenses that allow you to use those images in blog posts. iStockPhoto.com and Shutterstock.com are two of my favorites. However, before you use any stock images on your site—and encourage people to pin those images—you should check your stock photo site's terms of service to make sure they're okay with your using their images on Pinterest.

The rules of stock image sites are in flux right now. While stock photo houses are likely to get on board with the power of Pinterest very soon, it's a good idea to double-check with your service of choice in the meantime—just in case.

You should also consider freshening up the images on old blog posts, or going back through your blog archives and adding photos to your photo-less archived posts. You never know when an old blog post could gain big traction on Pinterest, so you want to make sure that every archived post—even the ones that are several years old—has a compelling photo published with it.

Nester Smith, who publishes home decorating blog The Nesting Place (thenester.com), found out firsthand that she needed to keep her eye on her old blog posts—and that they can be a surprisingly consistent (and lucrative) source of traffic for her site. In September 2011, Smith noticed some unusual things happening on her blog. Affiliate sales from an ebook she promotes on her site had doubled virtually overnight. When she investigated where all the new sales were coming from, she realized that one of her previous blog posts—one that had been written eighteen months prior, that featured a personal story and a link to that ebook—had gone viral on Pinterest. Pinners were sending an avalanche of traffic to her website, resulting in mounting ebook sales.

And that traffic continued to come in. During the month of November 2011, Pinterest users sent 22,000 visitors to that blog post. And Smith's sales continue to grow; in fact, sales of that ebook from her site are over $500 every month, as of this writing.

The moral of this story is: Don't neglect your old blog posts. You never know when an old article or web page will gain new life in the world of Pinterest!

Advertise Your Presence on Pinterest

Once you've got your account up and running and have published some boards and pins, make sure to let your website readers know you're on Pinterest. You can add a prominent "Follow Me on Pinterest" button to your website to advertise that you're a pinner. You can either use the free button that Pinterest gives you on their website (see all the Pinterest goodies at pinterest.com/about/goodies), or you can have your web designer create a special Pinterest button for you.

Where should you put your Pinterest badge? There are three main spots I recommend.

1. Placing your button in one of your blog or website's skinny columns (i.e., sidebars).

2. Integrating the button into your banner design.

3. Including the badge with the links to your Facebook, Twitter, or YouTube profiles (as shown in Figure 7.1).

No matter where you decide to put it, the key is to make sure your Pinterest button is easily visible to website readers. Don't make people scramble around looking for this link to your pins and boards; make it as easy as possible for them!

Special Advice for WordPress Bloggers

If you have a self-hosted WordPress website or blog, you're in luck. There are some great Pinterest tools for WordPress that you can use to make your site even more pin-friendly.

FIGURE 7.1 Pinterest badge options.

Pinterest RSS Widget

You can feature thumbnail images of your recent pins in your website sidebar by using a Pinterest RSS widget. Each thumbnail is a direct link to that pin's URL, which can help you get more followers and get your website users to engage with you on Pinterest. And it's a cool visual addition to your WordPress site, as well. You can get the RSS widget for your website by installing this WordPress plugin, as shown in Figure 7.2 (www.wordpress .org/extend/plugins/pinterest-rss-widget).

"Pin It!" Button

As a WordPress site owner, you also have a quick and easy way to add a "Pin It!" button to the footer of each of your blog posts (Figure 7.3). This button allows your readers to quickly and easily share your content on Pinterest. There are two options for "Pin It!" button plugins:

1. The "Pin It!" Button (www.pinterestplugin.com) installs a very simple button that just says "Pin It!" to the footer of each of your posts. Your readers can just click the

FIGURE 7.2 A WordPress Pinterest widget, powered by RSS.

button to pin any image from your post to one of their boards.

2. The similarly named "Pin It on Pinterest!" button looks nearly identical, but also provides a count of how many people have pinned your post. This plugin also gives you the option to select the image from your post that will get pinned when your readers click on the button, and allows you to enter a pin description. Your readers will have the option to change that description if they wish; however, many will just use the description you entered. This can

FIGURE 7.3 A blog post with social media sharing options in the footer, including the all-important Pin It button.

be a great opportunity to subtly mention your company, add more information about the product featured on the pin, or connect with Pinterest users. It's available at www .flauntyoursite.com/pin-it-on-pinterest.

Visual Blog Post Footer

You can add a visual prompt at the end of each of your blog posts that directs the reader to check out some of your previous related content. The plugin is called LinkWithin (www .linkwithin.com/learn); when it's installed, it will add a footer that features images from old content to your blog posts. Each thumbnail image in the footer is a link to a previous blog post, and LinkWithin serves up those old posts by searching for related keywords in the text of the article. If you've got compelling images in those posts, people will follow the links, check out your great post, and then pin the images to their boards.

Now that your website is all spruced up and ready for Pinterest users, let's talk a bit about how to nurture the relationships you're developing with your Pinterest followers.

Your Action Plan

- Get in the habit of adding images to each and every blog post or article on your website or blog. Check out stock photography websites for great images (making sure to verify that you can use those images on Pinterest).

- Freshen up archived or old blog posts with interesting, pin-friendly images.

- Install a "Follow Me on Pinterest" badge or button for your website, making sure to put it in a prominent place.

- Install a "Pin It" button in the footer of every page or post on your website, so your readers can easily pin your content.

8

The Care and Feeding of Pinterest Followers

We've already discussed the basics of connecting with other Pinterest users in Chapter 5. But how can you begin to deeply connect with your followers and fans on Pinterest in a way that inspires fanatical loyalty in them? That's what this chapter is all about.

The key to taking care of your followers on Pinterest is leveraging what Tara Hunt refers to as "whuffie." Hunt explains in her book *The Whuffie Factor*:

> *Whuffie is the residual outcome—the currency—of your reputation. You lose or gain it based on positive or negative actions, your contributions to the community, and what people think of you. The measure of your whuffie is weighted according to your interactions with communities and individuals. So, for example,* [my whuffie is higher] *in my own neighborhood, where I have built a strong reputation for being helpful, than when I travel to another neighborhood where nobody knows me.*

It's important to keep in mind when using Pinterest that you're building social currency as you publish content and interact with other users. You need to strike a constant balance between promoting your own material and publishing good resources, links, and images.

Picture your whuffie as a bank account: You need to make lots of deposits so that you have some currency to pull from when you need to make a withdrawal. If all you do is make withdrawal after withdrawal, you're going to run out of currency *fast*.

Companies and brands on Pinterest who only pin links to their own websites again and again won't develop whuffie—and therefore won't have successful pinning campaigns. But if a Pinterest user maintains a good balance between pinning promotional images and other content, they've found their whuffie sweet spot.

There is no exact formula for success on Pinterest, just as there is no equation or algorithm that guarantees success on Twitter or Facebook. But if you keep your ideal client in mind (remember the suggestion and ideas from Chapter 3), you'll start to get a good sense for how much promotion is too much. Put yourself in your ideal client's shoes when you look at your boards. Ask yourself: Would I want to look at pin after pin of ads, coupons, and other promotions? Or would I like to see compelling images, interesting resources, and inspirational photos? Would I like to see content that makes me trust the pinner who published them?

Build your clients' confidence and build your whuffie, and you'll find that your audience begins to know, like, and trust you.

There are many steps you can take to build your social currency and take care of your followers on Pinterest.

Take the Time to Authentically Interact with People

We've talked in previous chapters about a number of ways for you to interact with other Pinterest users. Make sure you're using those techniques appropriately. You also want to take good care of the mailing list subscribers you get from Pinterest by sending them *quality* content every month. Don't spam your subscribers, and don't sell their email addresses to other groups or businesspeople who want to spam them.

Be Open to Feedback

Allow your customers to submit ideas and give feedback to what you're doing online—on Pinterest, your website, and other social media sites. Ask them questions about your industry: What do they like? What do they hate? What would make their lives easier in this area?

I've seen some incredibly successful blog posts (on Copyblogger, Problogger, and other sites) that essentially ask their readers, "What is your biggest question about social media/ blogging/content marketing?" One such post on Copyblogger got over 300 responses! Remember that your readers want to tell you what is on their minds, and what is bugging them. They want to be heard.

Consider sharing a similar open post on Pinterest (or on your blog, with links to your pins or boards). Ask people to submit questions, inquiries, or pressing problems that allow you to better understand what's going on with them. If you want to up the ante a little, you could always offer a prize for a few randomly selected commenters, such as a half-hour of free consulting or a small free gift. This can be a fantastic technique for getting some new clients as well as gathering valuable data on the issues with which people are struggling.

Then make sure that you use that information to shape your business strategy. Utilize it as fodder for new blog posts, Pinterest boards, new products, workshops, or free reports. When your current and potential customers know that you truly understand their problems—and that you are doing your best to help them—they will buy everything you put on the market.

Embrace the Chaos

One of the biggest fears businesses have when they start blogs, Facebook pages, or Twitter accounts is that they will lose control of the public conversation. They are terrified of what people will say on their websites and social media pages.

There is no way around this. In many ways, you *do* lose control of the conversation. But look at it this way: Like it or not, people *are* talking about your business online. Would you rather be aware of people's comments (both good and bad) so that you can respond to them—or stick your fingers in your ears and pretend that no one is talking?

The key to being able to relax in social media is to embrace the chaos. Social media sites like Pinterest are not about keeping control of every image, every comment, or every remark on the web. They are actually about relinquishing some control to your customers. And it's entirely possible that people may say things you don't like. But if your users were complaining about you, wouldn't you rather be able to address it directly and respond? I know I would!

If people have valid complaints about your company that you are finding on Pinterest—address them! Reply to them, apologize for the mistake or problem, and ask what you can do to remedy the situation. Don't ignore negative feedback! Addressing the issue is *always* better than pretending you don't see problems at all.

Agility and flexibility are key characteristics for any business that wants to build community via social media. So take a deep breath, let go of those reins a little, and be prepared to surf the crazy waves of the interactive web.

Look for more suggestions about ways to engage with your Pinterest followers in Chapter 11, and use those suggestions as a starting point for your own brainstorming. You and your team know your audience better than anyone else, so you'll be able to think of great ideas for interacting with your Pinterest followers and other online fans.

Getting more engagement in your pins will make you feel better about what you're doing, too. Nothing is worse than publishing lots of great content and feeling like no one is listening—like you're just yelling into the void. People commenting and interacting with you gives you more motivation to keep going!

Getting More Pinterest Followers

Many of the suggestions from this book will naturally and organically help you build a following on Pinterest. Remember: The quality of your Pinterest audience matters a great deal more than the quantity. But if you're looking for some active ways to try to build your list of followers, here are five ideas:

1. **Follow other pinners.** This one sounds incredibly basic, but it truly is the quickest and easiest way to build a following. Many of the people you follow will follow you back, and your numbers will grow.

2. **Pin consistently.** If you pin every day, your numbers will also go up as more people repin, "Like," and comment on your content. So set aside a little bit of time each day to do some pinning.

3. **Actively seek out (and pin) new and interesting content.** The more original you are, the more followers you will get; so make an effort to find new things to pin (from your website and other online sources) instead of just repinning things.

4. **Link your Pinterest profile with your other social media accounts** (e.g., Facebook and Twitter). Check out Chapter 9 for more details on doing this.

5. **Run contests.** I'm not a huge fan of using this technique *all* the time, but it can give you a boost in your followers count. I would rather see businesses build their Pinterest bases more slowly by publishing great content, but I think an occasional contest is okay. Check out Chapter 11 for more information on running Pinterest contests.

■ ■ ■

Curation

One effective way to take care of your followers, feed them great information, and build their trust in you is to curate the very best content in your niche, and present it to them in easy-to-understand, organized, appealing ways.

What is content curation? Beth Kanter of BethKanter.org (@kanter), social media consultant for creative nonprofits, defines it in this way:

> *Content curation is the process of sorting through the vast amounts of content on the web and presenting it in a meaningful and organized way around a specific theme. The work involves sifting, sorting, arranging, and publishing information. A content curator cherry picks the best content that is important and relevant to share with their community. It isn't unlike what a museum curator does to produce an exhibition: They identify the theme, they provide the context, they decide which paintings to hang on the wall, how they should be annotated, and how they should be displayed for the public.*[1]

Being a content curator means that you pick the best stuff on the web—the most compelling images, inspiration, resources, and ideas—then thoughtfully organize that stuff in a beautiful way for the benefit of your core audience. You select all the best pieces of what you're learning, researching, and collecting, and wrap it all up with a lovely bow for your readers and followers.

So how does this pertain to Pinterest? The Pinterest model gives you the flexibility to create groups of content, organized under any topics you like, and then craft beautiful collages of your curated content for people to enjoy, learn from, and savor.

---

[1] www.bethkanter.org/content-curation-101.

Pinterest gives you a visually engaging foundation from which to build the museum of your curated thoughts and ideas.

Different fields and industries will have different trusted curators, and every board on Pinterest can be its own mini collection of curated content. Jodi Ettenberg (@jodiettenberg) is a former lawyer currently traveling (and eating) her way around the world. Jodi curates information on space on her super-cool board called "Space is Awesome." She uses her Pinterest board to collect images of outer space, the Northern Lights, stars, and the moon. The end result is a visually stunning collection of photos that is a pleasure to view and learn from.

So what kinds of boards could you create for your ideal clients?

Let's say that you run an animal shelter, and want to create separate boards for cat, dog, and rabbit lovers who are looking for the best information on their favorite animals. You could carefully select only the best training ideas for dogs, the best resources for building a rabbit hutch, and the best way to keep your cats from being bored in a big-city apartment. By carefully and diligently adding to those boards every day, your pet-loving followers will start to rely on you for the most reliable, up-to-date, well-vetted content on your topics.

By practicing great content curation, you'll become a trusted expert. And I can think of no better way to build a following than to take care of your Pinterest fans in this way.

So instead of thinking in terms of individual pins—and worrying whether or not you should pin one particular piece of content to a board for your business—picture yourself as the smart, savvy, discerning curator for your own online museum. Let your community in to see the best of the stuff you have gathered together for them; they'll be able to tell by the quality of the exhibit that you put each collection together with great care. They come to the museum because they want to learn from you. They want to take a break from trying to sift through the constant onslaught of new information out on the web and figure out what is important (and what is not). They trust you to tell them what the best and most critical pieces of information are in your industry.

Pinterest gives you access to all these possibilities and opens up a world where your ability to become a filter and aggregator for information can make you a highly valued and highly sought-after expert in your field.

Blogger Robin Good of www.masternewmedia.org shared this commentary on why content curation is important:

> *In a world where attention has become so scarce to become as valuable as currency, and where quality information on a specific topic requires ever more time and attention to be found, the value that* [curation could] *provide those who have the ability to organize, select, compile and edit the most valuable information on any one topic is incommensurable.*[2]

Staying focused on curation when using Pinterest has enormous potential to build your business following (which helps you financially, in terms of getting leads and sales). However, it can also help you attract a powerful like-minded community to your boards and pins. Sean Carton of social media marketing blog ClickZ (www.clickz.com) says this:

> *It's the "community" part that's at the heart of the whole curation movement and the most powerful element when it comes to curating content as a way of drawing traffic and attention in your marketing efforts. Just as a carefully curated museum exhibit is sure to draw like-minded people together, carefully curated content on the web has*

---

[2] www.masternewmedia.org/content-curation-why-is-the-content-curator-the-key-emerging-online-editorial-role-of-the-future/#ixzz1p97SopNW.

the potential to attract (and/or build) an online com-munity of people who are into the same stuff.[3]

The following are some examples of great curators on Pinterest:

Beth Kanter: @kanter

Jodi Ettenberg: @jodiettenberg

Kelby Carr: @kelby

Pinterest for Business: @pinterestbiz

HubSpot: @hubspot

Mikinzie Stuart: @mikinziestuart

And here's a tip from Rex Sorgatz of fimoculous.com to keep in mind as you begin the process of curating content for your audience: "The role of a curator is to find the most interesting things within this massive onslaught of messy information."

For more suggestions and ideas about content curation, go to www.bethhayden.com to download the *Pinfluence* supplemental materials.

Now that you understand how to take good care of your Pinterest followers (and add to the followers you have), let's move on to talking about the symbiotic relationship between Pinterest and other big social media sites.

Your Action Plan

- Authentically interact with people on Pinterest—get feed-back, participate in discussions, and listen to what your ideal clients are saying.

---

[3]www.clickz.com/clickz/column/2104954/content-curation-king.

- Use the feedback and ideas you get from your Pinterest interactions to shape the content on your blogs, YouTube channel, Twitter stream, Facebook page, and Pinterest profile.

- Consistently and thoughtfully curate outstanding content for your Pinterest followers and other online supporters.

Twitter, Facebook, and Your Blog

How Pinterest Plays Well with Others

Pinterest can be a fantastic tool for cross-publishing content with your other social media sites, including your blog, Facebook account, and Twitter profile. Luckily for users, Pinterest founders came up with lots of clever ideas for integrating the Pinterest platform with other social media tools, so there are many built-in ways to incorporate your pins into everything else you're doing online.

This chapter provides my best tips for integrating your Pinterest profile with your other social media tasks.

Social Media Strategy

It's worth revisiting your existing social media strategy before you start integrating your Pinterest account with your other social media profiles. Keep in mind the principles we covered in Chapter 3 by asking specific questions like: Who do you want to attract to your business? How exactly can you do this? You want to keep your messaging and attraction strategies consistent across all your social media efforts.

So—what are you currently doing with your Twitter, Facebook, and LinkedIn accounts to connect with clients and build relationships with them? Look at how you're already gaining traction with your customers on these social media tools, and try to replicate those themes with your Pinterest efforts. Sending a haphazard message to your prospects is going to work against you rather than for you. So figure out what's working in your social media activities—and what's not—to decide how Pinterest fits in.

That said, you always want to show some personality in your pins! Travel blogger Jodi Ettenberg (@jodiettenberg) loves marshmallows, a fact she highlights on her Twitter and Pinterest profiles. She has a Pinterest board (which she co-curates with three other pinners) called "For Marshmallow Enthusiasts" that features funny, quirky, and delicious-looking images of the sugary treats (Figure 9.1). Jodi's board completely works with her brand and her voice on the web, because her website and social media presence always features her delightful and open personality. People follow Jodi because they like *her*.

Marshmallows work for Jodi. What can you fit into your social media strategy that will help you show your personality and let your followers into your world?

FIGURE 9.1 Jodi Ettenberg's quirky and fun board for marshmallow enthusiasts.

General Tips for Sharing Pins

Pinterest is structured in a way that allows you to Like (on Facebook), tweet, and email any pin—your own, or someone else's. Just click on any individual pin within a board, and you'll see a larger version of that pin. On the right side of the pin, you'll see some of your social media sharing options for that pin.

You have the option to take any of the following actions for a pin:

- **Like**—*Like this pin on Facebook.* Seemingly, using this option will publish a thumbnail of the pin to your Facebook followers (along with a link to the pin), however in my testing I've found that it doesn't work consistently. You can see that you have Liked the post on Facebook when you look at the pin, but sometimes it doesn't appear in your Facebook timeline.

- **Tweet**—*Tweets a link to the pin via your Twitter account.* Includes the pin description in the tweet (or at least as much of the description as will fit into 140 characters—after that, Twitter truncates the description).

- **Embed**—*Allows you to embed this pin within a blog post or web page.* We'll talk more about this later in this chapter.

- **Report**—*Reports the pin to Pinterest for review.* Tells Pinterest that this pin is inappropriate or violates the site's copyright rules.

- **Email**—*Lets you email someone a link to this pin.*

The ability to take these actions with any pin already gives you many options for sharing that pin to your other social media accounts. If you see a piece of content on Pinterest that would be interesting or educational for your Twitter or Facebook followers, it is easy to share using these options. So look for opportunities to publish great Pinterest content to your Twitter followers and Facebook fans using these sharing methods.

Four Ways to Use Pinterest with Your Facebook Account

Pinterest has incorporated lots of great tools that work with the Facebook platform, which means there are lots of ways to leverage pins in the Facebook world.

1. **Connect Pinterest with your Facebook timeline.** In Chapter 2, we discussed how you can connect your Pinterest activity with your personal Facebook profile. When you take this step (via your profile settings) you integrate your Pinterest account with Facebook's timeline feature. This means that any content you pin on Pinterest also gets published to your Facebook profile. And don't worry about overwhelming your Facebook friends with constant publication of individual pins; your images get grouped, so Facebook will publish a few at a time, in one collection.

2. **Liking Pinterest boards.** You can also "Like" the individual boards of other users. Simply click on the board, then click on the "Like" button right under the title of the board. You'll be prompted to add a note, which will be published on Facebook with your link to the Pinterest board. Liking boards in this way can be really useful for your business, because it allows you to share whole collections of useful resources with your audience on Facebook (and add your comments about why those collections are important).

3. **Publish pins to your business Facebook page.** I mentioned in Chapter 2 that there currently isn't a way to integrate your business Facebook page with your Pinterest

FIGURE 9.2 What a pin looks like when you share it on Facebook. You can share a pin to your individual Facebook account, or to a business page.

profile to have your pins automatically posted on Facebook. However, there is a workaround that allows you to manually publish your pins to your Facebook page when you're pinning using the Pinterest bookmarklet for your browser.

Before you pin a new image, log into your Facebook account, then click on the dropdown menu next to the word "Home" in the upper-right corner of your screen. You'll see several options for using Facebook as a page, instead of as an individual (Figure 9.2).

Once you've selected your business page, go back to the image you'd like to pin. Then, as discussed in Chapter 4, you can use your bookmarklet to pin your image. Select the board you'd like to pin the image to, add your description, then click on "Pin It!" You'll see an additional pop-up box come up for a few seconds after you pin your image. This box simply provides some options for sharing that pin on other social media sites. You have the option to view your pin, tweet it, or share it via Facebook.

When you're logged into Facebook as your business's page and you use this option, Pinterest will post your pin directly to your business Facebook page wall, as seen in Figure 9.3.

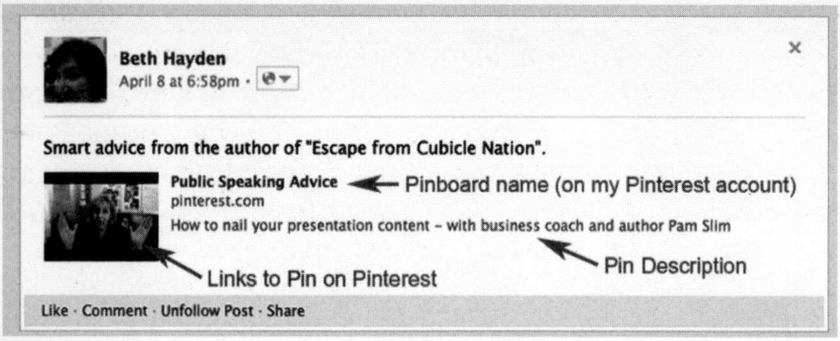

Beth Hayden
April 8 at 6:58pm · ⬚▾

Smart advice from the author of "Escape from Cubicle Nation".

Public Speaking Advice ◀— Pinboard name (on my Pinterest account)
pinterest.com
How to nail your presentation content – with business coach and author Pam Slim ↖ Pin Description

↖ Links to Pin on Pinterest

Like · Comment · Unfollow Post · Share

FIGURE 9.3   You have the option to share any pin via Twitter, Facebook, or e-mail.

Additionally, you can always post pins to your individual profile, too; it completely depends on the audience with whom you want to share that content.

I like to share blogging, Facebook, and Pinterest-related pins to my business Facebook page. If I think an image, video, or link will be interesting or compelling to my fans, I'll post it to my page. But if the pin I want to post to Facebook is about summer fashions, baby otters, or great recipes, I'll share it with my personal Facebook friends instead. I will typically share things with my business audience if I think they would be something my professional community would enjoy, and confine it to my personal network only if it's something my business network wouldn't get any benefit from.

Publishing Pinterest content to your business page on Facebook will help you build your page's popularity as well as your audience on Pinterest. It's a fantastic way to kill two birds with one social media stone.

Using Pinterest with Your Blog

The best way to use Pinterest with your blog is to discover who's pinning your blog material. We'll go into more detail about how to figure out what people are pinning—and how you can use it to your advantage—in Chapter 10. However, here's one quick trick: Go to www.pinterest.com/source/yoursitehere to see how many people have pinned content from your blog posts. For an example, you can check out all the different book covers and other images that users have pinned from Wiley Publishing's website by going to: www.pinterest.com/source/wiley.com.

By looking at your site's Pinterest source page often, you can discover which posts and images resonate most with Pinterest users, and use that information to shape your content strategy. For example, if you know that your posts about planning a budget wedding are taking off like wildfire on Pinterest, you'll know to write more posts about that topic—maybe articles on arranging your own flowers, cutting down on DJ expenses, printing budget invitations, and so forth. This kind of information is a gold mine for bloggers; you'd be crazy to ignore it!

You can also embed Pinterest pins into your blog posts. Just click on any pin, then click on the "Embed" button on the right side of the pin to get a code that you can paste into your blog posts to add compelling visual accents. You'll want to be very careful about copyright infringement when you embed content, however. I like to use my own content (e.g., mindmaps, company photos, etc.) when I embed pins into my blog posts, so that I don't get myself into any kind of legal trouble. See Chapter 14, "The Ethics of Pinterest," for more information on copyright issues when using Pinterest.

Using Pinterest with Your Video Marketing Campaigns and YouTube Channel

We've already discussed the fact that YouTube videos are pinnable within Pinterest, and that it's a great idea to pin your company's tutorials, how-to's, and behind-the-scenes videos to your Pinterest boards. If you're a social-media-savvy business, you probably already have your own YouTube channel that you use to upload useful and interesting video content that really speaks to your ideal client.

It's a great idea to create boards that feature your YouTube channel content in different ways. Consider creating a board for office videos, one for tutorials, another one for customer video tutorials, and so forth.

You can also pin any video that you think would be a good fit for your ideal clients, since videos make great selections for your content curation efforts as well. Refer back to Chapter 6, where we discussed good rules for content curation on Pinterest, to look for ideas about the kinds of videos you can pin.

You can ask a video professional how to add clickable links within your YouTube videos. When you do this, those links will be accessible when people play your video from Pinterest when it gets pinned by you or another Pinterest user, which may very well lead a good deal of traffic back to your site! Therefore, you want to be strategic about adding links to landing pages, great blog posts, or other content that's closely connected to your business.

Using Pinterest with Twitter

You already know how to tweet a link to a pin by clicking on it and using the social media sharing options to the right of every pin.

You can also tweet a pin after you publish it to a board using your Pin It bookmarklet. After you pin an image from any web page using the bookmarklet, you'll see an additional pop-up box come up for a few seconds. As stated above, this box simply provides some options for sharing that pin on other social media sites. To tweet it, simply select Tweet this Pin. You'll see a pop-up box that looks like Figure 9.4. Make any necessary modifications to the text of the tweet, then click "Tweet" when you are ready to publish it to your Twitter followers. Your completed Tweet will look like Figure 9.5.

You can also tweet the link to a pin manually. Every pin has its own unique URL (or *permalink*) that allows you to tweet any

FIGURE 9.4 How to use Facebook as your Pinterest page (great for getting more followers and engaging with other Facebookers).

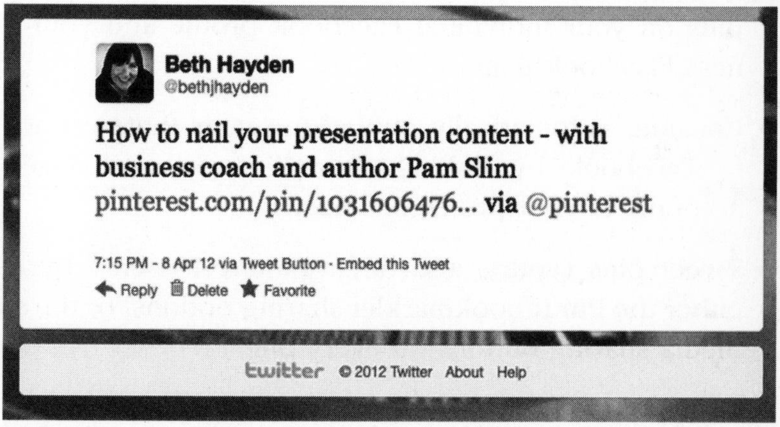

FIGURE 9.5 How to Tweet a pin in Pinterest.

pin whenever you like. To find a particular pin's unique URL, just click on that pin from an individual board, and then look it up in the web address field. Most pins will have a permalink that looks like this: http://pinterest.com/pin/103160647684466090.

To tweet a link to this pin, just copy and paste that pin's permalink and add it to your tweet, add whatever commentary you'd like to add, and publish the tweet.

Using Pinterest in conjunction with your other social media efforts (especially Facebook) can be great for your business. Think of Pinterest as another way to find and feature fantastic content for your blog, website, and social media profiles.

In Chapter 10, we'll talk about doing a little (legal) Pinterest spying. I'll teach you to monitor conversations on Pinterest and watch for trends, so your business is always on the cutting edge of what your clients and customers want and need.

Your Action Plan

- Familiarize yourself with all the ways you can link your Pinterest activity to your Facebook and Twitter profiles.

- Consistently cross-post your own pins (and the pins of other users) on Facebook by liking boards and sharing pins on your individual Facebook profile and your business Facebook page.

- Consider automatically publicizing your Pinterest activity to Facebook by linking your Pinterest and Facebook accounts in your profile settings.

- Tweet pins (yours, and other Pinterest users') by using either the Pin It bookmarklet sharing options, or the social media sharing buttons on every pin.

- Study what articles, images, and blog posts people are pinning from your website, and use that information to shape your content strategy.

Learning by Watching

Tracking Trends and Monitoring Conversations

Pinterest is a fantastic tool for gathering information from consumers and other businesses. You can learn a lot by watching what's happening within Pinterest; it allows you to keep your finger on the pulse of what people think about your company and about your industry, so you can be the first to jump on hot new trends that are just breaking in the online world.

All you need to do is learn some super-spy tactics so you can gather info by watching what's happening among Pinterest users, which is exactly what this chapter will show you!

Tracking Trends

Amy Clark, a popular blogger at MomAdvice (www.momadvice .com), keeps her eyes open for Pinterest trends and integrates those ideas into the content she creates for her blog.

I like to visit the "Popular" link on Pinterest to see what the most popular pins are . . . to help me brainstorm content for the site. [For example], when I saw that "mustaches" were trending on the Popular section, we developed mustache printables & Mustache Mug Templates[1] that our readers could use. Mustaches weren't necessarily a topic that I had planned to explore, but it worked out for us when the mustache fun hit Pinterest, and attracted new readers to the site.[2]

---

[1]www.momadvice.com/blog/2011/11/mustache-mugs-and-free-mustache-printable.
[2]http://momadvice.com/blog/2012/01/how-to-be-a-pinterest-superstar.

Pinterest can be the platform you use to observe and study our rapidly changing, highly responsive culture. And as a business owner, you can gather some truly priceless information by paying attention to what's happening on Pinterest.

Pinterest's "Popular" tab, which you can find in the top navigation of your Pinterest home page, provides a treasure trove of information about trending topics. Browse this "Popular" area frequently and take note of the kinds of things that are consistently showing up there. When you see a trend that applies to your niche, consider shaping your content strategy to include that trend; or use it to test possible products and services on that topic.

You can also look at your own pins (and those of the people you follow) to see what gets pinned frequently and what seems to be gaining traction because it's "sticky." Pay attention to what is grabbing people's attention—whether the content is yours or someone else's.

You can also perform searches in the Pinterest search box on your niche or topic. The search box is in the upper-left corner of most Pinterest pages. For instance, my recent search on "Pinterest Marketing" there resulted in a plethora of infographics, blog posts, and video about marketing using pinning campaigns. I can use this information to gain insight into what people are talking about, passing around, and saying about my topic. I can also see what questions are regularly coming up that I might be able to answer in my own blog posts and boards.

Keep in mind that many of the pins on certain topics are what marketing experts would refer to as "aspirational." Examples of aspirational content are things like: homes users would like to live in, recipes they would like to prepare, or big trips they would someday like to take. Looking at these aspirational boards can help you gain insight into people's ideals and values. What are they looking forward to? What is important to them? And, perhaps most importantly, how can your company help them do or obtain it?

For example, an adventure travel company like G Adventures (@gadventures) could gather information on what kinds of trips their target audience would like to take—and what their travel values are—by gathering data from Pinterest boards. They can use aspirational content from boards users publish with common themes like "Bucket List" or "Trips I Would Love to Take."

And remember those super-valuable ideal client profiles we've been talking about throughout the book? Looking at your clients' boards can really help you know more about your clients and what's important to them, which can help you fill in any missing pieces in those client profiles.

If you're watching trends carefully and consistently, you can be the first business in your niche to jump on new trends as they start to surface—and that gives you a major advantage over your competition!

Tracking Traffic and Conversions

Another way of learning and improving your business by watching on Pinterest is to carefully analyze your web stats. You can do this not only by watching your pins and boards on Pinterest, but by using your website traffic tracking program to figure out what kind of traffic you are getting to your website from your Pinterest efforts. Here are some things to try:

1. **Use Google Analytics** (or your favorite traffic-tracking tool for your website) to determine which pins and boards are bringing the most traffic back to your site. Popular bloggers always know what referring sites are sending them the most traffic, so they can maximize their efforts in online marketing. This is a critical part of engaging in Pinterest marketing, too. If you don't know how to look at your traffic stats or gather information like this, check with your web developer or social media guru to find out.

2. **Know which pins convert to mailing list sign-ups and purchases on your site.** Being aware of your conversion statistics is a critical part of this process. You can set up Google Analytics to run custom reports that let you gather information on particular queries, like "How many people who land on my site from a particular pin end up signing up for my website and buying my product?"

3. If you are driving traffic from your pins back to landing pages (to get visitors to sign up for your mailing list, or for special events like webinars), you can also **introduce split testing into your sign-up process**. Split testing is the process of improving your landing or sales pages by testing one version of the page against another and seeing which one performs better. Using split testing experiments, you can figure out what graphics, forms, and text work best on your pages.

    Because your Pinterest traffic does come to your website with slightly different expectations than other kinds of web traffic, it's a good idea to create Pinterest-specific landing pages that will appeal specifically to pinners.

    It's definitely worth putting some effort into improving your conversion rates. For more information on split testing, consult your company's web guru, or get in touch with us at Firefly Digital Marketing (www.bethhayden .com) for assistance.

4. **Find out what time of day and what day or days of the week you get the most repins, likes, comments, and referral traffic** by regularly analyzing both your Pinterest profile and your website traffic stats. Test out pinning on different days and times to maximize traffic and audience engagement. You may find that you get the most repins when you pin at 6 A.M., while others may find that evening pins work better for them. Once you know your peak Pinterest times, make sure you're making the most of

them and make every effort to ensure that you or your staff are pinning during those times!

5. **Once you know which parts of your Pinterest strategy are working, put that information to good use.** Use it to shape your visual content, decide the best times of day to pin, and keep tweaking your overall web strategy to continually improve your Pinterest results. Conduct a monthly assessment of your Pinterest marketing efforts to reshape and refine your strategy.

I know this sounds like a lot of work, and it can be. However, it's really worthwhile to try to uncover this information. You can also develop weekly and monthly checklists to make this kind of analysis part of your regular routine.

You should also be putting these tracking strategies in place for the rest of your social media efforts. Build these types of Pinterest analytics into your current social media reporting, and use ALL the information you gather to improve your entire online marketing strategy's results.

If you put these tactics to work on your Pinterest campaigns for six months, you'll be amazed at how quickly analyzing and using this data will make a difference in your business. You'll get more repins and more traffic, build better community, and make more sales. And isn't all that worth a little extra effort?

Tracking Impressions of Your Brand

There's an old saying in sales and marketing that goes, "Your brand is not what *you* say it is; it's what your *customers* say it is." So, find out what people are saying! This section will talk about the different ways that you can discover how people are talking about your brand, and what you can do with that information.

One of the quickest ways to start gathering data about online impressions of your brand is to look at your website's Pinterest source page and determine what types of content people are pinning from your site. It's one of the quickest and easiest ways to get a quick snapshot of what people value about your online content.

Every website that has been pinned on Pinterest has a Pinterest source page. To find your website's Pinterest source page, go to: http://pinterest.com/source/[yoursitehere]. For an example, the social media blog Copyblogger has a source page at: www.pinterest.com/source/copyblogger.com.

Look at your site's Pinterest source page often to discover which of your posts and images resonate most with Pinterest users. This information is incredibly important; by spying on the content that people are pinning from your site, you get insight into what is important to them (what they find useful, educational, or entertaining) and what they deem worthy of sharing with the world.

I have clients who are continually surprised about what gets pinned (and what doesn't) from their websites. Blog posts and images that they were sure would gain a lot of traction on Pinterest get no attention at all, while some obscure posts from two years prior take off like wildfire. It's important to take your judgments and preconceived notions out of the equation during this process, and instead look at what's *actually* happening.

You should regularly run searches for your company name and the names of your products and services in the Pinterest search box, as well. This is a great way of finding photos of people using your products—like books, household products, jewelry, and so forth.

While you're looking at pins about your company, whether they are on your source page or in other places, make sure to check the comments people leave on those pins. This can help you discover what is important to users about the images or videos they are pinning, and more importantly—how what they are pinning makes them feel.

Look at the ways that people perceive your brand. What are the names of boards your pins are getting pinned and repinned to? What types of images are users grouping you with? Are they putting you on boards like "Must Haves" or "Things I'll Afford Someday"? Looking at the names of these boards can help you gain an understanding of popular perception of your brand.

If certain Pinterest users are regularly posting photos of your products (on Pinterest or on their own blogs), you may want to consider reaching out to them and including them in any blogger outreach program you may already have in place. If you don't have a blogger outreach program, consider starting one, and integrating those efforts with your Pinterest marketing campaigns.

Getting Direct Feedback

One of the coolest ways to use Pinterest to watch and learn is to solicit direct feedback from your Pinterest followers and customers.

The Information School at Syracuse University (@iSchool) recently reached out to their readers by running an interesting contest. They published a post on their website asking readers to create a "Future of Librarianship" Pinterest board and collect their ideas on how to define the future of librarianship (Figure 10.1). Contestants submitted incredible boards for judging, and the iSchool picked the top eight boards and then let their blog readership select a final winner, who received a prize.

What a wonderful way to get feedback from people on their niche topic, get great exposure for the program's Pinterest profile, and build community. Brilliant!

You can gather feedback from your users in similar ways, whether online or offline.

For example, some companies are running Pinterest-based focus groups that they use to ask participants to curate boards on their industry (or other specified topics). They then watch as their participants add to and maintain these special boards.

You can also think about using collaborative boards with your focus groups to let people pin things as a group. If you choose to

FIGURE 10.1 One of the contest winners (@bkbiblio) for the Syracuse University School of Information Studies Pinterest contest about the future of librarianship.

do this, make sure people are prepared for the fact that whenever someone in the group pins something to the board, every board member will received an email (this could be either helpful or annoying, depending on the situation). We'll talk in more depth about working with collaborative boards in Chapter 11.

You can also use Pinterest as a de facto online laboratory by asking for feedback on upcoming ads, brand packaging, product names, or new product launches. How will you know if people love or hate the name of your new product? Ask them! People love giving feedback; if you set up your feedback campaign in an interesting or compelling way (or offer free giveaways or prizes to those who participate), it's possible for your feedback queries to gain some real traction online!

■ ■ ■

This chapter has taught you about the different ways that you can (legally) peek into your audiences' minds and gather data on what they think, what their purchasing decisions look like, and what is working (and not working) in your Pinterest campaigns. Keep in mind that Pinterest research like this is not a once-and-done affair; it's something that you must keep doing on an ongoing basis!

Develop a smooth, efficient process for gathering data; then make sure that the feedback and thoughts you gather from your customer make it back into your company strategy. It's like having your clients in your office with you, telling you what they really want and need. That information is incredibly useful, so make sure you're not wasting it.

Your Action Plan

- Keep your eyes open for Pinterest trends by regularly checking the "Popular" tab on Pinterest and watching for more trends in people's pins and boards.

- Track your website traffic and conversion statistics using your favorite web traffic tracking software.

- Consider trying split testing to increase conversions to sign-up and sales pages.

- Figure out the best times of day and days of the week for you to pin, based on Pinterest and website traffic data.

- Monitor conversations about your brand and consider soliciting direct feedback on Pinterest using focus groups or user-generated content on specific boards.

Part Three

Developing Pinfluence

Expanding Your Reach

How to Use Contests, Discussion Boards, Customer Testimonials, User-Generated Content, and Video Galleries to Get More Followers

So far, we've talked about the process of growing your Pinterest following by publishing great pins and boards, and taking good care of the followers you've brought to your Pinterest account. But there is a huge variety of other ideas for using Pinterest for marketing—ideas that I would call *black belt*, or more advanced, techniques. These ideas are for marketers who are comfortable with the basics of Pinterest and would like to expand their reach to get more followers, drive higher sales, and increase their customer engagement. You can pick and choose from the suggestions I make in this section, and implement the ideas that work for you. This is not meant to be a checklist; and not all of these ideas work in every situation. Once again, this section is best used as a way to kick off your brainstorming process, and think about all the possibilities you have for making Pinterest's visual content and social pinboards work for you.

Use Pinterest to Build Community

You already know the basics of building community, like engaging in conversation with your followers (and other Pinterest users) and curating the best possible content in your niche to establish yourself as a trusted expert in your field. The following are some more advanced ways of building community using your Pinterest boards.

Integrate User-Generated Content

More and more brands are setting up guest pinner programs for their Pinterest accounts, as ModCloth has done (Figure 11.1). Allow your best customers or star students (i.e., the people you

FIGURE 11.1   A ModCloth (@modcloth) board dedicated to guest pinners.

trust most) to join in on certain boards and encourage them to pin content for a week. Give them general content guidelines— make sure they're clear on who your core audience is, and the kinds of things your followers like—then set them loose to pin great content that your followers will find interesting. If you're a wedding venue, for example, your guest pinners could pin beautiful gowns, idyllic honeymoon spots or resources for planning a wedding on a budget. You'll be amazed what great content these guest pinners will come up with for you, and they'll be delighted to get more attention for their own Pinterest profiles. It's win-win for everyone involved.

Two quick notes about collaborative boards:

1. Pinterest has some serious limitations in the way their moderated boards are set up. When you invite someone to collaborate on one of your boards, the invitee doesn't get the opportunity to say yes or no, and is automatically added to your board. After that, he or she will receive an email every time someone pins something new to that board. This can be a major annoyance if the person you're inviting to co-pin isn't expecting your invitation. So make sure that you talk to your collaborators before you invite them, and explain what the Pinterest process will be like. You may even want to keep a template explanation for this purpose that you can cut and paste when you want to invite new people to collaborate with you.

2. The second disadvantage to the way Pinterest collaborative boards are set up is that there is currently no way to moderate joint boards—even when you are that board's owner or originator. If your guest pinner pins something you don't like and that you need to remove, you have to *ask* them to remove the pin from the board or remove that person as a collaborator altogether. This is yet another reason to consider your guest pinners carefully, and make sure you ask people you trust.

It's likely that Pinterest will fix both of these issues in future upgrades to their platform. In the meantime, collaboration boards are definitely still worthwhile—you just need to learn to work within their current limitations.

Create Holiday Boards

Celebrate the seasons by creating seasonal or holiday boards that relate to your brand (as in Figure 11.2). Examples: New

FIGURE 11.2　A holiday board from Pinterest user Amy Hanks (@aimmers).

Year's resolutions, Fourth of July, and the list goes on and on. Users love these!

Start Discussion Boards

Pediatric therapist staffing firm PediaStaff (@pediastaff) maintains ongoing discussion boards to engage with their clients and build community. They use a particular pin's description field to ask a question or pose a discussion topic, then use the comment fields to facilitate discussion amongst Pinterest users. For example, one week PediaStaff introduced a topic for occupational and physical therapists: great games to help with motor and sensory skills. This got a lively discussion going in the comments for that pin. This approach can serve as a fantastic engagement tool for current and potential clients, so think carefully about the kinds of discussions you could start for your Pinterest followers.

Host a Pin Chat

Career coach Sean Cook (@seanccook) hosted a unique online event that merged his Pinterest and Twitter worlds; he called it a "pin chat." It was part of a regular Twitter chat that he normally hosts for his audience, higher-education job seekers. Participants to the chat tweeted links and pins that featured quotes, videos, and other inspirational material for people seeking positions in higher ed (using a pre-assigned hashtag). Sean then re-pinned those items to one of his Pinterest boards. The event opened and closed at a particular time, as advertised on his website, www.higheredcareercoach.com. Sean's pin chat drew attention to the cool stuff that he's doing to inspire his clients using Pinterest, and provided a unique avenue for community-building that got people talking.

Spotlight Your Pinterest Community Members

Ann Handley and C.C. Chapman, co-authors of *Content Rules: How to Create Killer Blogs, Podcasts, Videos, Ebooks, Webinars (and More) that Engage Customers and Ignite Your Business*, suggest this approach for bloggers and other website content providers:

> *Create content that showcases your readers, viewers, commenters and other active members of your community. If you notice that Maisy and Simon consistently comment on your blog posts, for example, write a post thanking them; also point out who they are, and link back to their blogs or businesses. You might even highlight some of your favorite posts from their blogs. Bonus: Once you start highlighting your audience members, you might well spark more participation by others who hope that they too might get a spotlight shone on them.*

This great advice works for Pinterest, too. If you notice that certain users are frequently commenting and "Liking" your pins and boards, link to them, too. You can even consider creating a "Featured Pinner of the Month" board to highlight these super-users.

Connect Your Clients by Introducing Them on Pinterest

How about recognizing your best pinners by sending out a weekly "Best of Pinterest" email? The email could include spotlighted boards and pins from your clients' Pinterest profiles.

Create Boards for Your Fans to Express Their Support for You

The best way to handle this is to have a few board administrators whose job it is to repin the content from your fans. Think about things like videos, blog posts, or photos from your events. Give your fans a way to submit their content to you (via Twitter, Facebook, email, or blog post comment, for example) and make sure to include this submission information in the description of this board, so users know how to participate.

Advertise How Great It Is to Work at Your Business

Yes, this builds community, too! Companies like Accenture are even creating boards that advertise the advantages of getting a job at their company. Check out their "Careers at Accenture" board, aimed at attracting more women to join their ranks: www.pinterest.com/AccentureWomen/careers-at-accenture.

Create Boards for Conferences that You Attend

Before the event, you can write about the sessions you plan to attend and the people with whom you're hoping to connect, which is also a great way to promote other attendees! During the event, you can share photos and videos of sessions, presenters, and other attendees. You can also carry cards for conference attendees with instructions on getting invited to post on the event board; people will love the novelty of this approach. After the event is over, do some post-conference pins to share your follow-up actions and talk about what you're hoping to accomplish from the knowledge you gained and the people with whom you connected.

Use Pinterest as Part of Your Sales Cycle

You can use Pinterest as a way to attract leads and reach out directly to potential customers. Think about ways to integrate these pinning suggestions into what your sales and marketing teams are already doing.

Create Boards of People with Whom You Would Like to Connect

Business coach Tommi Wolfe (www.thestartupexpert.com) recommends that you keep a list of current professional contacts, as well as potential clients with whom you would like to connect. So why not keep this list on Pinterest? You could call it "People I'd Love to Know" and have those pins link to either that person's Pinterest account or to their main website.

Therapist and coach Tamara Suttle, whom I first introduced in Chapter 6, also maintains a "Favorite Pinners" board, which features her favorite users to follow on Pinterest. There's no reason that your favorite pinners board couldn't include potential clients you would love to land.

Run Contests

Businesses are starting to run all kinds of contests on Pinterest. You can invite your readers to pin links and images from your site that inspire, motivate, move, or entertain them. Or, you can ask them to create specially themed boards around your contest topic. Always make sure to promote the winners' boards on your website or contest board as part of the contest.

Keep in mind that it's a smart idea to craft a short, clear blog post that lays out the contest's rules and expectations. This will allow you to both advertise the event and be able to answer questions.

The following are possible ways to choose a contest winner:

- **Popular Vote:** Let the Pinterest public make the choice! Have the contest entrants create pinboards or special pins, then announce to the public that they can vote by liking or repinning the board or pin. The winner is the one who gets the most likes or repins.

- **Sweepstakes Entries:** Choose a random winner drawn from all the entries. Let entrants know what they need to do in order to enter—possibly repinning an image or following your brand on Pinterest.

- **Judging by Best Pin or Board:** Have users create a pin board that adheres to the contest guidelines; then you (or a panel of judges selected by you) choose the best one.[1]

- **Create Coupons and Pin Them:** Create beautiful, visually interesting coupons to add to your boards. You can either mix them in with your regular boards, if that feels comfortable to you, or create a special board for coupons and offers. Use coupons sparingly, though; you don't want to overwhelm your followers with too much directly promotional content.

Spotlight Your Testimonials

Pin pictures of your clients, and then paste their testimonials in the pin's description. People love seeing faces with testimonials; it makes them much more credible and friendly. This is

---

[1]http://socialfresh.com/pinterest-contests.

therefore another effective technique for gathering and sharing social proof about how awesome your company is.

Help Your Customers Visualize Exactly Who You Want to Work with

Remember when we talked about those ideal client personas in Chapter 3? Consider making them public!

Create a separate board to represent each client persona, and pin content to represent that type of client. This might actually make a great collaborative board with one of your best clients who fits that profile, too. You can then use those boards during your sales cycle to help your employees get a clearer idea of the kinds of clients you're trying to attract. You can link to this board from your website, on a page called "Who We Work With" or "Our Ideal Clients."

Engage with Your Referral Sources

Create boards for referral sources, affiliates, and strategic partners, and let them add to these boards. Engage with partners so they know they are included and appreciated. Better yet, *ask* these partners and referrers what kinds of content and boards they would like to co-create with you; I bet you'll get some fantastic answers!

Tell Client Stories

Pinterest gives you the ability to turn boring written case studies into dynamic, powerful visual success stories. Keep in mind that this is a little different than creating and pinning client testimonials. Testimonials are all about you and your company; how awesome you are, how you helped a particular client achieve a certain goal, and so on. But you can also create a board of stories that are focused on a variety of topics: how specific clients are using your product, what their lives looked like before they started working with you versus how much better they are now that you're helping them, and so forth. These can be incredibly inspiring and motivating stories for your other current and potential clients, too.

If you're a web design agency, for example, and you'd like to feature a current client's beautiful website (and all the great ways they're using it to market their own business) why not pin some of their posts and showcase their great site? You can also talk about their process for writing great blog posts, getting traction with social media, and so on. Think about how these stories will read to your potential clients; you want them to be moving and inspiring, and make other clients feel like they can take action and get results, too.

Use Pinterest to Help You Work with Current Clients

Pinterest has lots of potential for not only helping you get new leads, but making your life easier when working with current clients. These ideas will help you connect with people who have already purchased your products and services—and encourage them to continue to do so.

Create Quick-Start Guides or Owner's Manual Boards

Pinterest allows you to present your product documentation online in a way that new clients can easily access. Keep in mind that people who are purchasing your product for the first time may be a bit uncertain; therefore, you want to make this documentation fun and easy to read or watch.

If you're primarily a service provider, you can create a "How to Get the Most Out of Working with Me" board with ideas and suggestions on maximizing your service relationship.

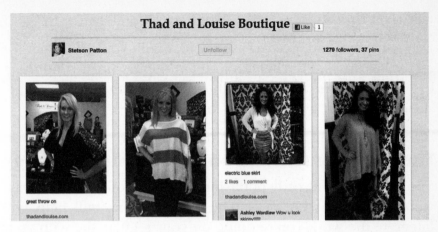

FIGURE 11.3 Boutique owner Stetson Patton (@stetsonkpatton) created this board to show off her boutique customers in their favorite outfits.

Spotlight the Ways Your Customers Use Your Products

For example, a clothing store or specialty boutique might take pictures of customers wearing outfits put together from their store. You could develop a whole board of customer photos like this; then make sure to link to those customers' Pinterest accounts in the description of the pin. The owner of Thad and Louise Boutique (@stetsonkpatton) in Hickory, North Carolina, is doing a great job with this technique (Figure 11.3).

Create Custom "Vision Boards" for New Clients

Your clients will be incredibly impressed if you create special boards just for them that include resources and ideas tailored to their individual situations. If you do this regularly—and well—it will really make your company shine.

This is a great technique for any business that relies on ideas or inspiration-gathering as part of their process with clients, such as wedding planners, interior decorators, caterers, and so forth.

Get Gift Ideas

Let's say that you need seasonal or thank-you gift ideas for referral partners, VIP clients, or other people who are important to your business. Check out those individuals' boards to get sneaky ideas for gifts they will love!

Use Pinterest to Build on Your Content Strategy

You're probably already publishing a blog or other content-rich website for your business. These suggestions will help you integrate the work you're doing on your regular site with your Pinterest efforts.

- **Integrate Pinterest boards with your blog.** You can create boards that are focused around your blog post categories. This is a great way to highlight archived posts and curate new content on that subject as well.

- **Write reviews.** Create pins reviewing products, apps, software, books, movies, websites, blogs, and other resources for your followers. This would be a great way to link to meaty blog posts that your followers will find really useful.

- **Utilize your video content.** Yes, you can pin video content! It's easiest to do on YouTube content—just use your Pin It! bookmarklet on any YouTube video page, and you can pin the main video from that board to any of your boards.

You can leverage any existing video content you've created and published (such as on your company's YouTube channel). Here are some ideas for video content:

- Customer testimonials.

- Speaking engagements and workshops.

- Industry events, meet-ups, conferences, and other gatherings.

- Webinars and teleseminars.

- Interviews with customers (ask them about their goals, about how they use your products or services, etc.).

- Employee interviews—Put your customer service reps in front of the camera. These employees have direct insight into the frequently asked questions of your customers and have great information to share.

- How-to content—video tutorials are powerful. Can you use how-to content via video to add useful pins to your boards?

Create boards for the classes and webinars you teach. These boards provide visually interesting and engaging supplemental material for your students. You can use them during your class or presentation, or send your students home with Pinterest boards to explore after class. If you're teaching a live class or workshop, be sure to include pictures from the actual event.

Whatever you do on Pinterest, keep the following tip from social media strategist Constance Aguilar in mind at all times: "Know what your fans like and give them more and more of just that."[2]

Hopefully this section has sparked some creative thinking for your company, and has gotten the wheels turning about all the different ways you can integrate Pinterest's tools into what you're already doing with your marketing strategy. Pinterest's beautiful interface and great content can really make you look like a rock star at all points in your sales cycle, so make an effort to use it every step of the way!

---

[2]http://alquemie.smartbrief.com/alquemie/servlet/encodeServlet?issueid=
3DE4CCD6-2091-4695-A7E2-6E7B64E4712A&lmcid=archives.

Your Action Plan

- Build community on Pinterest by gathering user-generated content, starting discussions, building conference boards, and so forth.

- Use Pinterest as part of your sales cycle by holding contests, pinning beautiful coupons, and publishing client testimonials and success stories.

- Work with your current clients using Pinterest tools by brainstorming ideas with client-specific vision boards creating tutorial content for Pinterest, and using other client-friendly methods.

- Make Pinterest a valuable part of your overall online content strategy by connecting your blog content with what's going on with your boards, creating robust video boards, and publishing supplemental materials for your classes and workshops.

Mobile Pinning

If you want to pin on the go, the Pinterest iPhone app is for you. It makes logging into your Pinterest account, pinning, uploading photos, and account management quick and easy from your iPhone or iPod touch. (As of right now, Pinterest hasn't developed an app for Android users, but I would bet that it will be in the works soon.)

Before we talk about specifics of using the Pinterest mobile application, it's a good idea to remind yourself *why* you're using Pinterest. As many of us know, nothing can suck energy from your marketing efforts quicker than a slick application that lets you waste seemingly endless amounts of time, while providing you very little return on investment, *if* you don't use it consciously and carefully.

The Pinterest iPhone app can very quickly turn into a waste of time for you if you don't remember why you're using it and who you're trying to reach with your pinning efforts. This might be a good time to revisit Chapter 3 to review your ideal client profiles. Remember what your marketing goals are before you even download the Pinterest app. It can help to (once again) ask yourself the following questions: Are you looking to grow your mailing list? Is your goal to create new and ongoing relationships with clients and potential clients? Do you want to increase interest and attendance at your live and virtual events? I'd even recommend putting your goals and ideal client profiles in a file on your phone. This way, you'll have those goals at your fingertips and, when you find yourself getting sucked into wasting time mindlessly on an app, you will always be able to remember why you are pinning and interacting on Pinterest in the first place.

Once you're clear on your reasons for using mobile pinning, it's time to get the free app. Download it by going to www .pinterest.com/about/goodies, or search for "Pinterest" in your phone's App Store.

But how can you use this great app to further your business marketing goals on Pinterest?

Ten Quick and Easy Ways to Build Your Business Using the Pinterest App

1. View and Share Images and Videos Pinned by the People You Follow on Pinterest

When you tap on the "Following" option at the bottom of the Pinterest app, you'll see the pins of the users you're currently following, so you can view them one at a time. You can scroll down a long list of pins and look at each one in turn. And the iPhone's clear graphics make the resolution of those pins excellent, allowing you to look at some very high-quality images.

You can repin, comment on, or socially share any of the pins of the people you're following.

2. Quick and Easy Community Building

Tap the "Activity" icon to see who has "Liked" and repinned your pins so you can follow them back. Tap the person's name to see the pin that user repinned or liked, then add your own comment to say thank you, ask a question, or get into a conversation with that person. You can also follow that person, which always helps build community, too.

3. Create Your Own Unique Pinterest Content

Snap your own pics from your Phone, and immediately upload them to your boards. When you tap on the camera icon at the bottom of the Pinterest app, you can take a photo and immediately upload it to your Pinterest account.

You can simply snap a picture, look at that photo's preview and make any necessary adjustments to the color balance and contrast of the photo by tapping and dragging within the image. Then when you're ready, just tap "Use." Pinterest will ask you to add a description, pick a board, and decide whether you want to add a place to this pin.

Not sure what kinds of photos to upload? Consider company events, staff photos, behind-the-scenes photos, product profiles, and happy customer images (with testimonials in the description areas). Refer to Chapters 6 and 11 for more ideas on the kinds of content you can pin.

4. Discover New Users to Connect with

Explore brand new pins from a variety of Pinterest users (not just those you are following) by tapping on the "Explore" option (Figure 12.1). You can choose a category you'd like to browse (Art, DIY & Crafts, Cars and Motorcycles, and so forth) or just touch "All" to look at pins from all categories.

Browsing this way allows you to see a variety of pins from users outside your typical Pinterest circles. This gives you the opportunity to curate information from a multitude of new sources instead of just relying on the Pinterest users to whom you're already connected.

Once you've chosen a category or tapped "All," you will see a selection of various pins on that topic. Tap on any pin to see a larger version of that image. Once the image has been expanded, you can see who the original pinner was, or tap on the image (or video) to check out its original source. If you scroll down slightly, you'll see more details on that pin, including the description, when it was pinned, and how many "Likes" and repins it currently has.

You can repin or "Like" the pin, just as you would in regular Pinterest.

FIGURE 12.1 The "Explore" view of the Pinterest App.

You can also:

- Comment

- Share on Facebook

- Share on Twitter

- Email a pin

5. See What You're Doing Right with Your Pinterest Campaigns

You can get a quick view of your boards and see which have the most followers. Tap the profile icon, then tap "Boards" in the upper-left area of your profile screen to get a quick peek. For instance, I can easily see that my "Blogging and Social Media Tips" board has the most followers of any of my boards. Then I can tap on that board to view its pins and see what I can learn from those images. What is it about that board that is causing a strong reaction from my followers? What makes it "sticky"? How can I apply this to my other boards to get more followers there?

6. Build Relationships

You can look at your recent Pinterest activity in two different ways within the Pinterest app. The first way is to look at the recent pins you have Liked in order to comment on or share them on social media. You can tap the profile icon, and then tap "Likes" in the upper-right area of your screen to view the pins you have Liked.

The second way is to tap "Activity" in the bottom navigation area to view a list of people who have recently followed you, repinned your images, or "Liked" your pins (Figure 12.2).

Thank people, ask them questions, converse with them in authentic ways—and above all, *listen* for feedback. The information you get from others will keep audiences coming back to your Pinterest boards—and getting new people to show up.

7. Curate Your Content by Repinning Interesting Things for Your Followers.

The "Explore" and "Following" functions in the Pinterest app let you easily browse through lots of new pins and continue your curation efforts. Additionally, the app's easy accessibility (and the fact that you have Pinterest on your phone, which you likely have with you most of the time) allows you to continue your curation efforts in small chunks during the day. Think about it: You can curate while you're waiting in line at the bank, waiting for a big conference call to start, or as a break from working on what you're focusing on during the day.

FIGURE 12.2 You can see recent Activity on Pinterest in the "Activity" view of the Pinterest App.

The app's convenience also means that you stand a better chance of being online and active on Pinterest during your peak times. (See Chapter 10 for more information on figuring out your peak Pinterest pinning time.)

Interesting images like Nester Smith's beautiful photo badges (see Figure 12.3) will be great sources of content for your curated boards.

8. Geo-Tag Your Uploaded Pins

When you take a photo from within the Pinterest app, you have the option of tagging the image using your current geographical location. Simply take the photo, as described above. You then

FIGURE 12.3 A single pin view on the Pinterest app (from Nester Smith, @nesters).

have the option to tag it with your current location on the screen where you select the board on which you'd like to pin that image.

Select "On" for the "Place" option on that screen, then tap "Pin It" (Figure 12.4). Your phone's internal GPS will calculate your current location and tag your photo with that location.

Here's why geo-tagging could be important for—and really help—your business: Pinterest may eventually reach the point where users can narrow their searches based on geographic location, similar to the advanced geographic searches you can run on Twitter. While Pinterest's search isn't sophisticated enough to do this type of search right now, it very well might in the future, and you want to be ready when it does. So tag your

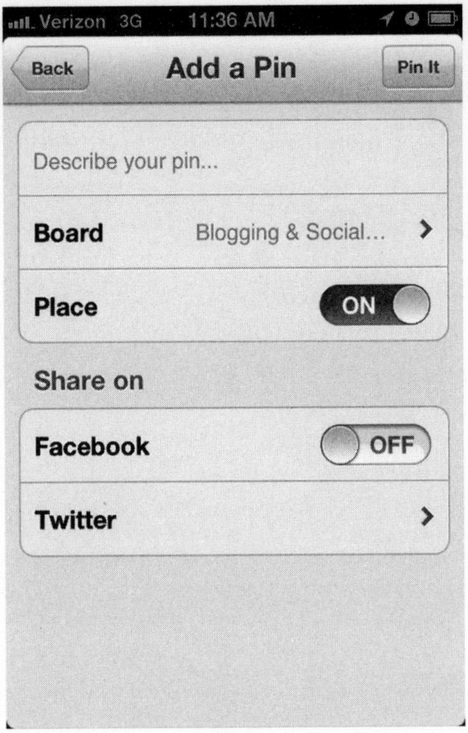

FIGURE 12.4 Your options when uploading a photo to Pinterest from your iPhone.

pins now; then when Pinterest releases that functionality, your pins will already by organized, sorted, and ready to go.

There is also some debate about how findable Pinterest pins are (and will continue to be) in Google and other search engines. But tagging your pins with your geographic location has some advantages if your pins will be findable in searches.

For example, let's say that you're in Portland, Oregon, and you run a regular Google search for the phrase "dry cleaner." Google serves up search engine results that are customized just for you; that is, dry cleaners that are close to you in Portland. Your result will differ widely from my results if I ran the same search in Boulder, Colorado.

While the technology is still growing, it might eventually be possible to have your pins and boards include geo-tagged information that people running Google searches in your area can access. This could potentially be a real boon for local businesses. The dry cleaner on Pinterest, for example, would be smart to geo-tag all of their uploaded pins; they *want* people to find their pins in their small town in Kansas when someone runs a search for "dry cleaner." Anything they can do to increase the likelihood that they will show up in the results when people run a search for their service in that town is a good thing!

A lot of the information on geo-tagging uploaded photos is in preparation for what might happen in the future. But since it only takes a moment to add a location to your pins, it's very easy to go ahead and do it.

The exception, of course, is if you are uploading personal photos (your house, your kids, etc.), and you don't want your location to be attached to the pin. In those cases, just choose the "Off" option next to "Place" when you're uploading photos.

9. Pin from Your iPhone Browser on the Go

You can also install a "Pin It" bookmarklet to your iPhone browser. This bookmarklet works exactly the way it does on your regular browser, so you can pin things when you're surfing the web on your phone. Check out these step-by-step directions for installing this mobile browser bookmarklet: www.pinterest .com/iphone/bookmarklet.

10. Pin from Your iPad for Larger, Crisper, More Beautiful Images

As of this writing, an iPad app for Pinterest is on the way. When it comes out, you can bet that you'll have a larger, more beautiful interface to do your mobile pinning. So make sure to keep your eyes open for the upcoming iPad app.

■ ■ ■

The beauty of using the Pinterest mobile app is the freedom it gives you to pin when and where you want, at any time of day. And the Pinterest app is also lots of fun. You get gorgeous views of beautiful pins within the Pinterest world, and the app's ease of use makes it fun to spend time on your boards and get a lot done in a short amount of time. So remember to make your smart phone a part of your Pinterest marketing strategy!

Your Action Plan

- Download and install the iPhone Pinterest app.

- Create a daily and weekly schedule for pinning and engaging with users using the app.

- Tag your uploaded iPhone photos with your current geographic location.

13

Pinterest for Nonprofits, Business-to-Business Companies, and Blog-Based Businesses

If you're trying to market a nonprofit or business-to-business (B2B) company, you may be thinking, "This all sounds great, but how do any of these suggestions apply to me? My company is such a unique, special-category business."

If Pinterest isn't a great fit for your business—if your customers truly aren't using it and you don't believe it's going to help you—that's fine. But since more and more companies *are* using Pinterest—and getting great results from it—don't dismiss it without researching it carefully. A recent survey by Price-Grabber found that that 21 percent of people on Pinterest have purchased a product after seeing a photo on the site, and you don't want to miss out on the action because you assumed Pinterest couldn't possibly work for your business.[1]

This chapter will give you some examples of particular types of companies and brands that are using Pinterest in really clever ways. These stories may spark some ideas for you—especially when you see the diverse businesses and nonprofits that are putting Pinterest to work for them.

Ask yourself as you read these examples: Are there ways to apply these ideas to my brand, products, and services as a B2B business? Or, if you're in a nonprofit business, can you use these ideas to connect with the people you're targeting as donors, volunteers, and supporters?

B2B Companies

PediaStaff, a national staffing firm that recruits and places pediatric therapists, is an unusual Pinterest success story. PediaStaff's

---

[1]www.mediapost.com/publications/article/171682/mccormick-dives-into-pinterest.html?edition=45352#ixzz1r68fiGTj.

clients are schools, hospitals, and clinics, and the organization's mission is to provide the very best qualified staff for their customers. PediaStaff is a great example of a business-to-business company that is thriving by using Pinterest marketing to foster relationships and build trust.

The company's team members use its Pinterest account to stay in touch with potential recruits and clients on an ongoing basis. They've found success in Pinterest marketing by using a creative mix of targeted visual content, interactive discussion boards, and consistent linking of Pinterest images back to its main website.

Based on their experiences on LinkedIn and Facebook over several years, PediaStaff has learned the value of sharing content as a way to build and nurture community, and develop relationships with potential customers and job seekers. They brought this same smart content-marketing mindset to Pinterest when they started using it.

As a quick refresher, **content marketing**, (which we first discussed in Chapter 6) means "creating and freely sharing informative content as a means of converting prospects into customers and customers into repeat buyers."[2]

PediaStaff actually has two audiences they need to reach with Pinterest. They have to connect with the hospitals and clinics who are their main customers, but they also need to build relationships with the job-seeking therapists they are trying to recruit. Pediastaff uses its Pinterest boards and pins to accomplish both of these goals.

When you land on the PediaStaff profile page, you get the immediate impression that they are doing something really different on Pinterest. The first two boards that you see on their profile page are "New?? Pls Start Here!" (a board that includes instructions on how to use the PediaStaff boards) and "Board

---

[2]www.copyblogger.com/content-marketing.

Announcements" (one that gives notifications of new boards, board splits, and other items of interest).

The rest of their boards are a treasure trove of resources and information for hospitals, clinics, and job seekers. These include discussion boards for school-based occupational therapists and physical therapists, and collections on ADD/ADHD, neonatal care, and music therapy. PediaStaff also features a board called "Pin/Pinboard of the Week," where they feature the best of recent content.

Everything about the PediaStaff Pinterest boards is focused on providing the very best content on the web (curated specifically for their audience) and facilitating discussion and dialogue with the people with whom they are trying to build relationships.

And PediaStaff's actions are paying off for them in very important ways. The company's interactive content manager, Heidi Kay, reports that the PediaStaff Pinterest account currently has more than 15,000 followers, and that Pinterest has become the biggest traffic driver to the company's website. Pinterest now drives three times as much traffic to PediaStaff's main site as their next-highest referrer, Facebook. PediaStaff has over 127 boards and 11,000 pins for their customers and job seekers to peruse, and they are undoubtedly known as the go-to expert in their field for information and resources.

How can you take cues from this B2B company's success on Pinterest? Here are some things you can do to make Pinterest work for you as a B2B company.

- **Build Pinterest into your current sales funnel.** How are you currently bringing clients to your website and blog? Are you using Facebook and Twitter? Driving traffic to webinars, teleseminars, white papers, e-books, or other free content? The best way to make Pinterest work for your B2B company is to leverage it as a traffic source that leads visitors to the ways you are currently collecting qualified leads. Link your pins to landing pages for your webinars and free e-books. Give content away graciously and generously on Pinterest, and lead the traffic you get as a result through your organized, frictionless sales funnel.

- **Showcase your company culture.** Your business has a personality, so make sure you're letting it come through via Pinterest. One of the best ways to use Pinterest is to humanize your company through pins and boards; it allows you to use your actual content to highlight the cool things about your company.

- **Spotlight those fantastic infographics.** We talked about this quite a bit in Chapter 6, but make sure you remember that infographics make great Pinterest content for B2B companies. If you're spending the money to have your design agency create those infographics, make sure you're getting maximum mileage out of them.

- **Add pins at conferences.** Create boards for conferences that you attend, and make sure you carry cards for other conference attendees that include instructions for getting invited to post on that board. Then ask those attendees if you can add them to your mailing list, too (and make sure you *always* ask!). Conference attendees will love being included in group boards for events, and you'll become quite the conference star as other people find out about your cool Pinterest conference board and start viewing your content as the go-to place for getting conference news, information, and photos!

- **Use content you already have.** Do you have ebooks or white paper covers from previous free content? Utilize those images on your boards, and use the description space to talk about the benefits that this great content can provide for your reader. You can then link those book covers to landing pages on your site where users can sign up to get that free content.

- **Pin with conversions in mind.** When you're pinning as a B2B company, it's important to use Pinterest with the goal of driving quality traffic to your website and converting your followers to paying customers. Keep in mind that Pinterest is another source of lead generation for you. Find situations in which it is appropriate to link your pins back to your website (to landing pages, webinar sign-ups, blog posts, etc.). Of course, you don't want to overdo this, because you want to mix your conversion-strategy pins with content that you're curating from other places. However, it's definitely okay to use Pinterest to drive traffic back to your site. So make sure you do so!

- **Pin client photos and testimonials.** One of the best things that B2B companies can do on Pinterest is pin client photos, stories, and testimonials. Pinterest users will love seeing your happy clients and getting ideas from them about different ways to use your products. And if you have clients on Pinterest, this is also a great way to help them build *their* following.

- **Spark discussion.** Take your cue directly from PediaStaff, and create discussion pins that are dedicated to starting conversations among your followers and customers.

- **Demonstrate practical use of your brand.** Can you show your customers what using your machines will look like in practical, everyday situations? General Electric (@general-electric), or GE, has an entire board called "Badass Machines" that is essentially a geek's dream (Figure 13.1). The board features pictures of GE machines in action, which gives Pinterest users a peek into all the different things that GE does, and how sophisticated their machines are.

FIGURE 13.1 General Electric's (@generalelectric) sweet "Badass Machines" Pinterest board.

For other ideas for B2B companies, check out what these businesses are doing on Pinterest:

- Mashable (@mashable)

- HubSpot (@hubspot)

- Constant Contact (@constantcontact)

As a B2B company, you *do* have different challenges than companies that sell their products and services directly to consumers. But Pinterest still holds enormous potential for you. Just remember that *all* companies are based on the same idea: **People selling to other people**, whether you're selling necklaces as a B2C boutique or consulting and widgets as a B2B company. Hopefully the ideas I've shared here, and the examples I've shown, have given you some ideas for building a Pinterest presence for your company. Feel free to let your creativity take over from here!

Nonprofits

Joe Waters, a marketing consultant for nonprofits who blogs at www.selfishgiving.com, wrote an insightful piece for *Huffington Post* about how and why nonprofits should engage with people on Pinterest. However, he urges the people behind these causes to consider some things before they start pinning when he writes:

> ***"Do you have an interesting or compelling story to tell with images?*** *Every cause does, but believing you do is half the battle. Pinterest is a natural site for museums, historical sites and cultural institutions. Maybe your nonprofit helps needy kids and you have a pinboard called 'happy moments' to capture all the great things you're doing for and with kids."*[3]

If your organization's marketing goal is to raise funds and reach out to donors, consider using the power of Pinterest's visual content to convey powerful and emotional stories. You want stories that stick, and Pinterest can help you tell them.

Consider the following great ideas for creative uses of Pinterest for nonprofits.

Animal Shelters and Animal Rights Organizations

Organizations that place rescued pets or fight for animal rights can create boards that feature their success stories. For example,

---

[3]www.huffingtonpost.com/joe-waters/why-how-causes-should-use_b_1190956.html.

the Animal Rescue of the Rockies (@arrcolorado) features heartwarming rescue and reunion stories of real pets and the humans who love them. Or what about vegan recipes from the People for the Ethical Treatment of Animals (@officialpeta)?

It's also a great idea for shelters to create boards for dogs, cats, rabbits, birds, and other pets that need permanent or foster homes. They could also curate great content on pet toys, training products, and healthy pet food.

Wildlands Network (@wildlandsnetwrk), an organization dedicated to restoring, protecting, and connecting wild places in North America, has a terrific board called "What We Do." A board like this is a terrific way to get your message across to your nonprofit's donors, volunteers, and other supporters, because it allows you to actually *show* them pictures of what you're doing in the world.

Environmental Organizations

There are great opportunities for Pinterest marketing for nonprofits that focus on environmental issues. If you have a big volunteer event, you can feature pictures of happy participants working together to clean up troubled areas, or create collections of inventive recycling efforts sponsored by your organization. Think community garden photos, school awareness-building talks, and videos designed to nudge followers to take action in their communities.

The Nature Conservancy (@nature_org) features a new "Green Gift" every Monday, where they highlight eco-friendly gifts from all over the web. (See Figure 13.2.) They also have cool boards for earth-saving recipes, a bird-of-the-month club, and winners from their annual photo contest.

Water.org (@waterdotorg), a nonprofit organization founded by actor Matt Damon and water-supply expert Gary White, has transformed hundreds of communities worldwide by providing

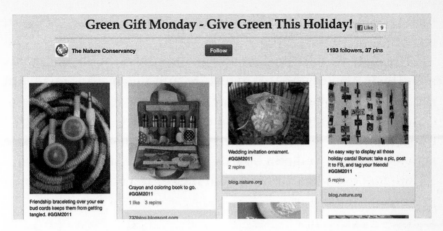

FIGURE 13.2 The Nature Conservancy (nature_org) features a new green gift every Monday.

access to safe water and sanitation. Their Pinterest board entitled "Water is Life" spotlights beautiful photos of water and the role that it plays in our lives. Its compelling images really drive home the point that access to clean water is a necessity for human beings everywhere.

Libraries

Library administrators and outreach teams are doing amazing things with Pinterest. Because Pinterest is such a great tool for curation, libraries use boards to collect and gather information on various topics that are important to their patrons, including information for parents, teens, history buffs, book club members, and many more. If you work for a library, you can also create visually interesting reading lists on a variety of themes, like staff recommendations, teen-friendly novels, summer reading, and so forth.

The Barrington Area Library (@balibrary) in Illinois has a total of thirteen pinboards. One called "Grow a Reader" features information and resources for parents and teachers who want to encourage children to become lifelong readers. They also maintain an extensive community resource board that lists local activities and library events.

The staff of the San Francisco Library (@sfpubliclibrary) is using their Pinterest boards to feature stunning historic images of the Bay area, including photos of the construction of the Golden Gate Bridge. Children's librarian Anne Clark (@sotomorrow) uses Pinterest in very creative ways to collect ideas for storytime activities, library bulletin boards, and folktale storyboard inspiration. She even has a board with ideas for a Star Wars-themed program at the library!

Museums, Zoos, or Gardens

You can create a shared pinboard that allows your visitors to pin their favorite pieces of artwork, zoo animals, or public garden plants. Or you might want to maintain boards of images based on the behind-the-scenes activities at your organization. What about a "Day in the Life of a Zookeeper" board? Your donors and supporters will love getting a special peek at what happens after hours at their favorite zoo!

The Cincinnati Zoo (@cincinnatizoo) has a board that features great pictures of their animals—even the smaller, often-overlooked creatures, like hedgehogs. They also have boards that provide details on zoo events, and they reach out to their primary client base by keeping a board that gives families some fun ideas for activities to do together (even including some that have nothing to do with animals or zoos).

The Chicago History Museum's (@chicagomuseum) boards not only feature incredible photos from many different time periods in Chicago history, but they also showcase beautiful images of weddings held at the museum. They even have a board that includes links to different items at the museum's cool gift shop.

Check out the New York Botancial Gardens (@nybg) and The Getty Museum (@gettymuseum) for more incredible ideas for showcasing your organization's amazing offerings.

Health Organizations and Hospitals

Pinterest has great potential for health organizations and hospitals that want to curate the best health-related content on the web. Diet and fitness advice, patient stories, and other content that connects you with your ideal clients are all great material for pinboards.

The marketing and outreach team at Dayton Children's Medical Center (@daytonchildrens) targets parents as their ideal clients. Therefore, their boards are packed with awesome parent-friendly recipes, stories, decorating, and crafts. One of my favorite Dayton boards is one called "Miracle Stories," which features fantastic photos of former patients. The descriptions of the kids' photos describe what their health issues were and how they are growing and thriving today. Seeing these now-flourishing children's smiling faces makes a pretty strong case for why parents should bring their kids to Dayton Hospital if they need medical care.

These examples have given you a variety of ideas for using Pinterest for nonprofit community-building and outreach. Keep in mind the other concepts we've talked about in this book—content curation, building relationships with your followers, building Pinterest into your overall marketing in smart ways—and you'll be on your way to success with Pinterest marketing for your cause or nonprofit organization!

For more ideas about using Pinterest for getting the message out about your cause, go to www.bethayden.com to download more nonprofit marketing ideas.

In Chapter 14, we'll wade into the somewhat complicated world of Pinterest ethics. We'll talk about how to protect ourselves as artists or visual content providers, and how to decide what to pin as business Pinterest users.

Your Action Plan

- Decide whether using Pinterest is the right decision for your B2B company or nonprofit.

- If yes, get your marketing team together and decide which of these ideas you'd like to put in place—or create your own new ideas!

- Track the success of your efforts on Pinterest, and refine your B2B or nonprofit Pinterest strategy as needed.

The Ethics of Pinterest

If you're a Pinterest user, then you're likely already aware of the firestorm of copyright controversy that has surrounded the site in the last few months. Because Pinterest grew so quickly—faster than almost any social media site in history—some of the Pinterest terms of service became problematic very quickly, too. Therefore, the site's founders have recently absorbed some heated criticism from bloggers and traditional media outlets about the use of images as shared content on their site.

I'll use this chapter to discuss some of those issues and give advice for content providers (artists, photographers, and so forth) who want to protect themselves online. I'll also share some of my observations about how businesses that want to engage in Pinterest marketing can keep themselves and their organizations out of legal trouble.

Please note that I am not a lawyer, nor someone with legal expertise. I am merely an observer and a user of the Pinterest process. This book does not contain legal advice. If you are looking for legal advice, please consult with an intellectual property attorney who can advise you on using Pinterest.

Advice for Artists, Photographers, and Other Visual Content Providers

I'd like to first address the concerns of artists, photographers, and other people who provide visual content on the web—folks I'll refer to as artists throughout this section.

As a quick aside about the Pinterest terms of service: Until recently, Pinterest *did* have a line item in their terms of service that stated that by using Pinterest, you were allowing the site to sell the images that you uploaded or to which you linked. Artists (justifiably) got very upset about this clause, and many complained. As of April 1, 2012, Pinterest removed the word "sell" from their terms of service, stating:

> *Our original Terms stated that by posting content to Pinterest you grant Pinterest the right for us to sell your content. **Selling content was never our intention and we removed this from our updated Terms.*** [Emphasis added.][1]

It's understandable that artists feel vulnerable about the use of their images on Pinterest; these are valid concerns. But there are steps that artists can take to protect themselves, while still enjoying all of the great benefits of having their images on Pinterest.

Being willing to loosen the reins a bit regarding your approach to sharing your content online can also have enormous benefits when it comes to Pinterest. Pinterest now drives more traffic to websites and blogs than Twitter, YouTube, and Google+. That means that millions of visitors are going to websites from Pinterest pins, and that some of those visitors could be coming to your site and purchasing your work.[2]

The possibilities for artists to monetize and benefit from this referral traffic are astronomical. So before you make major decisions about whether you would like to participate in sharing your images on Pinterest—and yes, this is a decision you can actively make—please make sure you are using all the facts available to you.

Trey Ratcliff, a photographer and blogger who wrote a now-famous post called "Why Photographers Should Stop Complaining About Copyright and Embrace Pinterest," takes a radical stance on how artists can relate to online sharing:[3]

---

[1]http://blog.pinterest.com/post/19799177970/pinterest-updated-terms.
[2]http://blog.shareaholic.com/2012/01/pinterest-referral-traffic.
[3]www.stuckincustoms.com/2012/02/13/why-photographers-should-stop-complaining-about-copyright-and-embrace-pinterest.

As this future becomes more and more plain to me, I see a rapture of sorts, where old-school photographers clinging to the old-fashioned ways of doing things will be "left behind." So much of the irrational behavior and anger is usually based in fear (fear-of-change, specifically), but it doesn't have to be that way.

When it comes to sharing your photographs online, you can go in two directions. You can put small images online, watermark them and then spend some or all of the week chasing down people that have used them inappropriately.

Or, you can be like me.

Offer up all your creations . . . to the will of the web. The web, and the universe, has a certain flow to it. You can become one with that flow and enjoy the ride. You can let the opportunity of what-can-be motivate you rather than the more poisonous fear-of-loss.

Yes, Ratcliff's opinions are pretty far to the left of norm, and yes, he has taken quite a bit of flack for this public expression of his ideas. But Ratcliff's open sharing policy is paying off for him. When he wrote this blog post in February 2012, Ratcliff reported that he had received over *35,000 unique website visitors from Pinterest* in the previous month. That is *a lot* of traffic.

If you make the decision—as an artist and content provider—that you do not want your images shared on Pinterest for any reason, you can take certain steps to lock down your photos and report offending Pinterest users so they remove the images that are up on the web. However, if you want to take a page from Ratcliff's book and open yourself up to the world of business benefits that can come with sharing your images on Pinterest, the following are some things you can do to protect yourself and your images, so that you receive proper credit for your work.

- **Keep your images at a fairly low resolution (72 ppi) and a smaller size.** Don't upload or use huge images (greater than 2500 pixels wide) on your website. The larger an image is, the more likely it will be used in ways you don't want it to be used. So keep them small.

- **Put your attribution in the pin's description.** If you are pinning your own work, include your name, a copyright symbol, the work's name, and your website address. Make sure to include the http:// at the beginning of your site address, so it becomes a live link in the description. A typical attribution would look like this:

  ©2012 Beth Hayden, *Title of Artwork,* http://www .yoursitehere.com.

- **Watermark every single image.** Whether you're publishing your images on your own website or you plan on uploading them to Pinterest, one of the best safeguards you can put in place is to watermark the image with your name and/or your website (or preferably both). Some artists disagree with this point; they're reluctant to add a watermark to the edge of an image, because they think Pinterest users will just crop the watermark out. I have also heard of artists refusing to add a watermark to the image's center because it interferes with the overall look. However, I highly encourage you to add your watermark to the bottom or top edge of the photo in a large enough font that it is easily readable on Pinterest.

  Believe it or not, the vast majority of Pinterest users either don't know how to crop images or will not take the time to do so. I have worked with hundreds of people in my online marketing business in the last five years, and I can say with absolute certainty that most people just don't know how to crop images. So don't worry so much about people taking the time to crop out your watermark. In all likelihood, your watermark will stay on that image everywhere it goes on Pinterest.

- **Monetize your website.** This is the "don't get mad, get paid" school of thought for artists. If you're an artist or photographer on the web, and you don't yet have a seamless, fast way for your site visitors to buy your work from your website, then you need to remedy that immediately. Set up a shopping cart to sell your prints, or an affiliate store where you can recommend products to your readers and visitors and make a commission on what you sell. You can also set up an Etsy shop, which will give you a slick and easy online store and help you process credit cards easily. Etsy is a marketplace website for craftspeople and artists who create handmade or vintage items—they allow you to create your own shop and sell your wares online. Whatever you need to do to get yourself on your way to making money with your website—do it *today*.

    You want to ensure that you can leverage the traffic you get from Pinterest into cash in your pocket. You are missing out on a *huge opportunity* if visitors who arrive on your site don't have an easy way of buying your gorgeous work. I feel passionately that any artist should get a shopping cart or other means of monetization in place, even before establishing the rest of the marketing suggestions in this book.

Protecting Your Copyright

If you don't want your images being used on Pinterest—or if you discover that someone is using your images illegally—you *do* have options for controlling the use of your work. Pinterest will support you in taking down pins that violate your copyright. Here are a few things you can do:

- If you find that your images are being used on Pinterest in a way that you don't think is legal or attributed fairly, you can either: 1) ask the pinner via a message (in the image comments) to link the image to your website (and preferably a sales page on your website where visitors can buy prints or other versions of the image); or 2) ask the pinner to remove the image completely. Usually Pinterest users will be more than happy to oblige either request.

- You can also use the Pinterest pin-reporting process to report the pinner if they refuse to comply after you write to them. The Pinterest website states:

  Every pin is accompanied by a "Report Pin" button, and users who discover infringing content can file a complaint with Pinterest through its Copyright Infringement Notification form. The notification requirements include a URL to prove that the content is your own, the URL to the infringing pin, your name, and home address.

  Find out more (and get the notification form) by going here: www.pinterest.com/about/copyright/dmca.

- If you decide after considering your options that you don't want anyone pinning images from your website, you can add a small piece of code to your site that will block Pinterest applications and bookmarklets. You can get the details here: http://blog.pinterest.com/post/17949261591/growing-up.

- If you want to add an extra layer of protection, and your site is built on a self-hosted WordPress platform, you can also install this plugin, which blocks readers from downloading any images from your site: www.wordpress .org/extend/plugins/no-right-click-images-plugin.

Advice for Business Owners, Nonprofits, and Bloggers Using Pinterest for Marketing

Pinterest's terms of service make it clear that users are responsible for making sure they don't violate the copyright laws of other content providers. The terms state:

> *Pinterest values and respects the rights of third party creators and content owners, and expects you to do the same. You therefore agree that any User Content that you post to the Service does not and will not violate any law or infringe the rights of any third party, including without limitation any Intellectual Property Rights . . . publicity rights or rights of privacy.*

When addressing the use of images that belong to other people, The Copyright Act states that you may not reproduce or distribute photographs that you don't own. In a nutshell—a Pinterest pinner needs to obtain permission from the person who holds copyright of each image that he or she pins. This obviously puts Pinterest in a very difficult spot, given that its business model is based on people being able to pin content freely from the web, and repin content that they find interesting from other people's boards.

Debate is raging all over the web about this problem. Some users have deleted their boards due to fears of lawsuits and retribution. There is a lot of confusion about what the right thing to do might be.

A copyright or intellectual property lawyer will recommend you do the following if you market your business on Pinterest:

1. Pin only your own images and videos, or images from artists who have given you permission to publish their work within Pinterest.

2. Read all agreements (with artists) carefully to see where you may need to attribute credit to the artist, as well as

getting permission. If their permission requires you to give a written attribution, make sure to do it clearly in each description.

A recent statement from Pinterest, however, hints at the fact that they believe they (and their users) have some degree of protection under the Digital Millennium Copyright Act (DMCA). Their statement reads:

Pinterest is a platform for people to share their interests through collections of images, videos, commentary, and links they can share with friends. The Digital Millennium Copyright Act (DMCA) provides safe harbors for exactly this type of platform. We are committed to efficiently responding to alleged copyright infringements. We are regularly improving our process internally with the help of lawyers who are experts in the field of copyright.

As a company, we care deeply about creating value for content creators. We're spending a great deal of time reaching out to content creators to understand their needs and concerns. So far, we've received overwhelmingly positive feedback and have created both tools for publishers who want to make it easier to pin their content (the "Pin It" button for publisher sites) as well as tools for those who would prefer that their material isn't pinned (an opt-out code that content owners add to their site that prevents content from being shared on Pinterest).

Our goal at Pinterest is to help people discover the things they love. Driving traffic to original content sources is fundamental to that goal.[4]

---

[4]www.washingtonpost.com/business/technology/pinterest-addresses-copyright-concerns/2012/03/15/gIQAijAFES_story.html.

So where does this leave you, as someone who wants to use Pinterest for building their business and creating community? Should you: 1) delete your boards, 2) pin only your own images, or 3) create collections of images from all over the web? Only you (and your lawyers) can come to a final conclusion on that. However, I believe it is worth taking a careful look at all the issues involved before fleeing Pinterest, as some would have us do.

As a frequent Pinterest user and observer, I feel comfortable sharing observations about how people are trying to pin in ethical ways. Some users feel that they can still collect images from the web, but do their best to make sure their pins link to the original source of the image, and that artists and other content providers are given every opportunity to monetize their beautiful work.

Ethical pinners, as many call themselves, always do the following:

1. **Pin to original sources for photos.** When pinning content that is not theirs, ethical pinners do their absolute best to make sure that the images they pin link back to their original sources.

   Responsible pinners are equally careful when they repin images. Users take an extra moment before hitting the "repin" button to find the original source of the image, in order to link it to its proper owner.

   There's one trick you can use to find an image's original source: right-click the image in the pin and select "Copy image URL." Then go to http://images.google.com and click the camera icon in the search bar. Paste your image URL, click on "Search," and browse through the results until you find the image's original source.

   You can also use the reverse image source TinEye (www.tineye.com) to determine the original source of an image.

2. **Pin with attribution.** Ethical pinners are sure to include information about the original content provider in the description of the pin (see instructions above about how to do proper attribution).

3. **Do not argue if they are asked to take down pins.** If artists or content providers ask them to take pins down or reattribute images, ethical pinners do so pleasantly, quickly, and without attitude.

4. **View Pinterest as an opportunity to build business relationships.** Success in business—whether online or off—is built on a solid foundation of relationships and community. Ethical pinners believe it is their duty to go about their business in ways that are fair and decent—and that part of that is to support other artists and content providers by doing their best to drive targeted traffic to their websites or blogs. Encouraging artists, photographers, and content providers to monetize their Pinterest traffic whenever possible is also the right thing to do. Businesspeople helping businesspeople is a powerful model.

What Now?

So, what will happen next for Pinterest, with regards to copyright issues? I asked Attorney Jonathan Pink—who heads the Internet and New Media Team at the law firm Bryan Cave—how he thought current problems around Pinterest copyright would shake out, considering what happened with similar situations in the past with sites like Facebook and YouTube. He answered:

Facebook is different because they only use a thumbnail on [Facebook], (which then links to the original site). The courts have ruled that is not infringement. In fact, that is one easy way that Pinterest could correct the current situation, although I doubt it would work with their form of content delivery. Absent some technological advancement that would allow for such thumbnails, Pinterest will either be sued into oblivion a la Napster, endlessly settle copyright claims (and take down images) a la YouTube, or so few authors will bother to sue the individual pinners (due to cost, low return-on-investment for cost-of-suit, and apathy), that it will continue on more or less as it is. I'm betting that there will be a lawsuit against the site that causes it to morph somewhat. I can't predict what it will look like three years from now, but I will predict that it will not truly succeed . . . until it works out some of these fundamental issues.

There's also the chance that Pinterest may work out some sort of arrangement that *isn't* on Pink's list—some fourth possibility that no one has thought of yet. The wild and wooly world of online user-generated sites (and the copyright issues that follow them) will continue to grow and change, and it seems likely that changes in our copyright law may follow. In the meantime, though, our job as Pinterest users is to figure out the approach that works best in our individual situations.

Your Action Plan

- Talk with your attorney about the issues surrounding Pinterest, and decide what your Pinterest business strategy will be.

- Be the most ethical pinner you can be in all situations.

Conclusion

So, what happens next?

This book was designed to get you thinking about the myriad of ways you can use Pinterest to market your business. I hope that now that you've finished reading, you can get started with some of the action items listed at the ends of the chapters.

And the Pinterest marketing excitement doesn't end here—I'd love to connect further! The conversation continues at my website (www.bethhayden.com), on Twitter (@bethjhayden), and, of course, on Pinterest (@bethhayden).

I'd love to hear how the ideas in this book have inspired or helped you. Tell me how Pinterest has expanded your business and helped you connect with your customers, and you might be featured on my blog or on my Pinterest boards as a *Pinfluence* success story!

And as a parting gift, don't forget to pick up your supplemental Pinterest materials at www.bethhayden.com. Just click on the Pinterest logo to download your free reports, ideas, and checklists.

About the Author

Beth Hayden is a social media specialist and technology trainer who helps entrepreneurs make money effortlessly through Internet marketing systems that support them every step of the way. Beth has been a featured guest blogger at Copyblogger.com and Problogger.com, two of the web's best social media and blogging sites. Beth is routinely invited to speak at industry events, including as a panelist at the Bulldog Report's PR University panel on Pinterest Marketing and PR. She lives in Boulder, Colorado, with her son.

Get more *Pinfluence* free reports, checklists, and marketing ideas at Beth's website, www.bethhayden.com.

Acknowledgments

This book would never have happened without the unflagging support of my friends, family, and colleagues.

Special thanks to:

Andrea Meyer, for painstakingly reading every chapter of this book and offering not only fabulous proofreading but thoughtful commentary and encouragement.

Mindy Brooks, for her cheerful and enthusiastic early support of this project, and my High Council of Jedi Knights, for their early advice and words of wisdom.

Corinne McKay and Bethany Siegler, for keeping me company on long workdays, and helping me think through how to present my ideas in helpful ways. You guys keep me on track.

Kristina Holmes, the world's greatest agent, for jumping headfirst into a project moving a hundred miles an hour, and for speaking slowly and using small words to explain even the toughest publishing concepts to me.

The great folks at John Wiley & Sons, for seeing a great idea for a book and helping me bring it to life on the page.

To all the gals of Boulder Media Women, for helping me give my business wings and cheering me on while I wrote this book.

Lori Wostl, for consistently telling me to "Go For It," and then figuring out how to help me do anything I want to do.

Toby Rogers, for helping me figure out the toughest chapters with your calm voice of reason and your crazy-smart brain.

For Michelle, my friend and greatest strategic partner, for recognizing that I could do great things long before I did— and for seeing the light, even when things get really dark.

Mom, Dad, and Amy, for having faith in me and encouraging me, even when my plans seem truly crazy.

Ben, for being the forever light of my life. You save me every day, kiddo. This book is for you.

Index